"Destined to be a classic in the canon of mountaineering literature."

—Peter Kick, Author of *Desperate Steps: Life, Death, and Choices Made in the Mountains of the Northeast*

"Anyone reading this book will take a little bit of Kate with them. The strength and poignancy of her story builds in a fashion similar to the storm she encountered."

—Perry Williamson, First female Outward Bound instructor on Hurricane Island, and Sterling College artist

"Gagne adeptly integrates a tale of high adventure gone awry with the intriguing science behind the risks and decisions we as humans face. Within this finely-crafted account, the various threads comprising this story are seamlessly interwoven against the rugged backdrop of New Hampshire's Presidential Range. Matrosova's fateful solo journey hauntingly unfolds alongside an analysis of the dire climatic and geographic elements conspiring against her. The daring rescue efforts undertaken to save her are so viscerally penned as to transport readers right to the wind-tortured peaks being contended with. *Where You'll Find Me* serves as an example of just where decisional missteps can lead us—and a sobering reminder of Mother Nature's deadly potential."

—Edward Swanson, Award-winning author of *Mesmer's Disciple* and *Madoc's Legacy*

"Gagne's analysis of Kate Matrosova's final climb is an outstanding case study on how a series of miscalculations and bad luck, rather than a single event, can lead to tragedy—even for the brightest and most accomplished among us. In the vast majority of the operations Global Rescue performs every year, it is the former, rather than the latter, that leads to unfortunate outcomes."

—Daniel L. Richards, Founder and CEO of Global Rescue

Where You'll Find Me
Risk, Decisions, and the Last Climb of Kate Matrosova
Copyright © Ty Gagne 2017

ISBN: 978-0-9962181-5-3

TMC BOOKS LLC
731 Tasker Hill Rd.
Conway, NH 03818
USA
www.tmcbooks.com

Where You'll Find Me

Risk, Decisions, and the Last Climb of Kate Matrosova

Ty Gagne

Foreword by Caroline Alexander

For Kate and Charlie

For the rescuers

A Note on the Title

It's Nov. 4, 2016, and I'm at the Mount Washington Hotel in Bretton Woods, N.H., a majestic resort that sits at the base of an even more majestic set of mountains, known as the Presidentials, within the White Mountain National Forest.

I'm standing at the podium with Chief Alan Clark of the Sugar Hill Fire Department. Chief Clark is the founder of the all-volunteer Pemigewasset Valley Search and Rescue Team (PVSRT). He invested his own money to start the team after recognizing the need for such services in the region. Dressed in his Class A uniform, he is cutting a fine figure at this event, the annual dinner hosted by North Country Public Safety Foundation, an organization that provides assistance to public safety officers and their families.

Clark is one of this organization's founders as well, and I am the guest speaker. There are 300 people in attendance. I was invited because, for more than a year, I've been doing a presentation called "Trouble in the Presidentials: What a mountaineering accident can teach us about decision making and managing risk." The presentation is centered on a tragic 2015 incident involving thirty-two-year-old Kate Matrosova. It can be scheduled into a sixty-minute session or expanded to a full-day workshop. For this event, I've been given a "firm" twenty minutes to speak, and I cannot use the audiovisual technology that normally anchors the story. Challenge accepted.

Prior to my presentation, Chief Clark and I talk about some of the details of Matrosova's death. Though his team was not involved in the rescue effort and eventual recovery, he is well versed in the incident. During our conversation, he offers this poignant thought: 'When [Matrosova] hit that emergency beacon, based on everything I've read and everything I've heard about her, I don't think it meant, 'Please come save me.' She knew it was the end, and she did it for the rescuers. She meant, 'This is where you'll find me.'"

That is the moment the title for this book was born.

A view of Mount Adams on the left and Mount Madison on the right, with Madison Col in between, taken from the south.

Contents

Foreword

In the early morning of a bleak winter day in February 2015, Kate Matrosova, an experienced and exceptionally fit climber, arrived at the Appalachia trailhead parking lot in New Hampshire's White Mountains to embark upon an ambitious but carefully researched and planned traverse of the Northern Presidential Range. The weather was not as fiercely cold as she had anticipated, and although forecasts told of big weather coming, the omens looked good for her plan, which would have her back to warmth and safety by 6:00 p.m. that night. The roughly fourteen-hour winter trek was to take her over five peaks, culminating with Mount Washington, whose 6,288-foot height, although low by mountain standards, routinely experiences some of the highest wind speeds on earth and some of the worst weather in the world.

At 5:10 a.m. on this day, meteorologists at the Mount Washington Observatory posted an online forecast that warned of a developing weather system predicted to deliver wind gusts up to 125 mph. But these conditions were hours away, and Matrosova planned to be down the mountain and back in her car before the weather broke. In her carefully constructed plan, moreover, she had identified six bailout points, routes by which she could safely abort her traverse, and which would take her down below the tree line if she ever felt she was in over her head.

Matrosova's carefully selected gear reflected her desire to travel light and move quickly. In addition to food, water, and layered winter clothing, she also packed an Apple iPhone, a Garmin Global Positioning System, a satellite phone, and an ACR ResQLink Personal Locator Beacon. And yet despite detailed weather forecasts and the battery of space-age technology she carried, Matrosova would not survive the day, and the highly experienced and motivated rescue teams dispatched, on ground and by air, would not save her.

Ty Gagne, a risk management authority and certified Wilderness First Responder with wide climbing and hiking experience in the White Mountains, was haunted by Matrosova's story from the time he first heard it. And the more he learned about Matrosova—her remarkable journey from Siberia to the United States, her talent and discipline and many accomplishments—the more haunting the story became. How had her last venture ended so badly?

Drawn to research Matrosova's tragic last journey, Gagne found himself analyzing her options at every critical junction, trying to assess at what points she could have still saved herself, and at what point things had gone irreversibly, fatally wrong. In *Where You'll Find Me*, Gagne takes the reader on this same quest as, with clear-eyed investigative research and unwavering compassion, he follows Matrosova's last climb, step by step and hour by hour. His own experience in the same mountains had taught him how easy it is to make small errors, and how these seemingly small errors can mount to threaten safety. Gagne's intent was to learn from Matrosova's journey, to see the choices she made, before and during the hike, to understand how and why she made them, and to share the insights.

Stories about survival serve to inspire us, and we are drawn to them like moths to a lighted window; they demonstrate that the human spirit can rise above what appear to be unbeatable odds. Many of the most inspiring of these tales come from the last century, when explorers set out armed with what seems to us today to have been shockingly inadequate equipment and advance information. Such stories not only inspire but can also be instructive, and we subject them to close scrutiny for the wisdom they can impart. But also instructive are the opposite of these stories, which demonstrate that sometimes—often—even indomitable spirits may not prevail. Terrain, wind, weather—the forces a climber faces today—are as severe and uncompromising as they were when earlier explorers faced them a hundred years ago. As severe, too, is the risk for human error. Possibly, some essential survival skills are more difficult to hone and sustain today than they ever were before. To what extent, for example, does an iPhone loaded with music distract from situational awareness? To what extent does a welter of information about weather and expected conditions create the illusion of control? And to what extent does carrying the means to call for help instill the false sense of security that, once requested, help can in fact be extended?

In its detailed exposition of Matrosova's journey, *Where You'll Find Me* offers both a tribute to a brave spirit and a master class in risk assessment and the so-called soft skills that will always be needed to survive. It also serves as a bracing reminder that, even equipped with twenty-first-century technologies, those who venture into the world's wild places today are as vulnerable as the explorers of old.

Caroline Alexander
June 13, 2017

Prologue
FULL CONDITIONS

"Climbers experience the consequences of their actions immediately and on a personal level."
—Reinhold Messner, mountaineer, explorer, and author

The Franconia Ridge
White Mountain National Forest, New Hampshire
February 2008

I was in trouble. Not the kind I was in when, as a new driver, I was stopped for speeding and, rather than issue a ticket, the officer called my father before I arrived home. No, this was the kind of trouble where I was placing myself and the people I was with at risk. At the invincible age of sixteen, I had ignored the speed limit. A little more than two decades later, I was ignoring my own limit.

In retrospect, the trouble began for me as soon as I awoke that morning. Low visibility outside, the cocoon-like microclimate of my warm bed, and a stout westerly wind pushing against the bedroom window were combining to create a contradiction in sensory stimulation. Was this really a good day to hike the Franconia Ridge traverse? It was not. Red flag number one.

Then I thought about my level of physical fitness for the challenging trip ahead. Marginal at best. Red flag number two. And was I sure I wanted to spend a long, grueling day with two guys I had never met, let alone hiked with? No, not feeling it. Red flag number three.

As I considered what to do, I allowed myself to suppress that initial grasp of the obvious—my rational acknowledgment that today wasn't the day to get after it—in the interest of preserving my ego. I was not going to be the one to back out, so I rolled out of bed to prepare for the hike I'd committed to: a winter traverse of the Franconia Ridge with two people I didn't know, while out of shape, and in what would surely be described as adverse hiking conditions. Somehow I knew that those first red flags would not be the last of the day.

"Honey, it looks really bad out. Are you sure about this?" asked my wife, with the perfect balance of anxiety and empathy. I don't think I responded with anything more than the clenching of my jaw, avoidance of eye contact, and a "Yep, I'm good."

Not long afterward, my ride pulled into the driveway, and I collected the gear I'd set out the night before. I hadn't skimped, and the load was heavy. The weight of the gear would further challenge my already mediocre level of fitness. Still, I'd figured, better safe than sorry. I introduced myself to the vehicle's sole occupant, whom I'll refer to as Greg, as I loaded my gear into the back, and we made the quick trip over to the next town to pick up the third member of our team, a man I'll call Dave.

I'd gotten connected to Greg and Dave through my wife, who knows Greg's partner. My wife learned that Greg and his friend were going to do a traverse of the Franconia Ridge that weekend. While I had been on Mount Lafayette many times in winter, and often in high winds, I hadn't done the 2.8-mile traverse of the narrow, exposed ridge that connects the Appalachian Mountain Club's Greenleaf Hut with Mount Haystack. But I had always wanted to. Although I had never accompanied them before, I knew these two guys had a lot of winter experience. They were close friends who climbed ice and took long outdoor trips together, and I sensed strong backcountry chemistry between the two that I didn't share. My experience level wasn't much different from theirs, but the trust they had in each other was based on shared experience and easy camaraderie. We would get along fine, but our newly formed threesome lacked the relational bonds of their established friendship.

The ride north was quiet. There was the usual winter whoosh of wind buffeting the car, nudging it from side to side as if the driver were drunk. He wasn't, but I recall wishing I were a little bit buzzed, just to take the nervous edge off. Up in the front seat, my companions chatted, and their easy relationship reminded me of the bond I shared with my climbing partner, Ron. In that moment, I wished he were there. If he had been, I know I would have felt more relaxed. I had moved to the back seat when we headed north, and my silence during the drive meant I wasn't engaging. It's not that I didn't like these guys or that they were shutting me out. It's just that my own "stuff"—my mental baggage—was getting in the way. I felt I had something to prove to them, something they already knew about each other, and that made me uncomfortable. So, I found myself chiming in here and there, much like an awkward teenager trying to make conversation with the cool guys.

We arrived at the Lafayette trailhead, parked the car, and retrieved our packs. Downed branches and other debris littered the parking area, the wind was crazy loud, and I couldn't see the summits or the ridge because they were so socked in. "Hmm... full conditions," deadpanned Greg, whom I'd also perceived to be the trip leader, maybe because he was the driver.

Packs on, we started moving. No time to waste, too cold to linger. The weather that day on Mount Washington, not far from where we stood in Franconia Notch, told the day's story:

Maximum temp: 27°F

Minimum temp: 6°F

Average temp: 17°F

Average wind speed: 61.1 mph

Maximum wind speed: 118 mph

Had I checked the weather leading up to departure? No. Did I ask Greg or Dave if they had checked the weather? Still a no. Was the weather in the parking lot bad? You bet. I wanted to go home. By that time, I had already lost count of the red flags.

The start of Old Bridle Path is quite flat, and I felt good weaving through snowy woods, crossing partially frozen streams, and staying close to the other two. But as the inevitable inclines appeared, things started to change for me. Greg and Dave were moving at a pretty good rate, faster than I normally would have, even at a higher level of fitness. It was relatively early in the day, and I was already pushing myself, with steeper and more challenging terrain ahead. Not hydrating, not snacking, not good.

I soon fell behind, but my companions were still in sight. The gap between us was now both perceived and real. I'd already burned more calories in ninety minutes than I'd burned in any exercise all winter. I was laboring up the steeper sections of the approach to Greenleaf Hut. High on the trail, close to tree line, the wind erupted in a cacophony of violent sounds. This felt dumb. This now felt wrong.

I arrived at the hut, which had been boarded up for winter, shortly after Greg and Dave. They were layering up out of the wind, hydrating, fueling, and making small talk. I added a jacket but didn't bother to have anything substantial to eat or drink. The quick break was over. No time to linger. Our advance toward tree line and the Mount Lafayette summit continued.

The walk from Greenleaf Hut to tree line is really quite beautiful, and despite my struggle to keep going, I couldn't help but admire my surroundings. Across a frozen pond and into a thick patch of spruce trees, I enjoyed a brief interlude of splendid isolation, even with partners near.

But once we arrived at tree line and into unprotected terrain, reality bit again. I've never skydived, but if I had to imagine what it's like, I think it would have a lot in common with what I was experiencing at that moment. Standing at tree line and preparing myself to continue onward felt like standing in the doorway of an airborne plane. The wind, like a thousand bitterly cold hands, was forcing an unwelcome, deep-tissue massage on my back, my entire right side—and my brain.

It wasn't long before I fell farther behind. On occasion, I lost sight of my companions, who were making great haste to get up and over the backside of the summit and out of the strongest wind gusts. It's impossible to re-create with any coherence what I was thinking and feeling at that point. I had turned into a mass of sensory perception: wind high; visibility low; body cold and tired. I was losing confidence at every step. And I was feeling stupid.

Finally, I tagged—or rather "grazed"—the summit of Mount Lafayette which, at 5,260 feet, is the highest peak along the Franconia Ridge. We had climbed almost 3,500 vertical feet to get there. On many days, the summit more than rewards the work, offering a stunning view of the Pemigewasset Wilderness Area. But on that day, there was no view, and wind gusts forced us to hurry off and take shelter behind a rock formation on the leeward side of the peak.

Even there, the wind was too loud and the air too cold to chat. Greg asked me for my camera and took a picture of me. I had one glove off and a look of pure misery on my face. When I saw what the photo exposed, it made me angry. I looked done, cooked, defeated. In fact, I was so upset with what I had revealed that I deleted the image a few days later. Had to preserve that ego.

I wanted to turn around and go home. I definitely did not want to traverse the narrow, exposed, wind-battered ridge. But I said nothing to Greg or Dave. Given the strength of the southwest winds, I'm not convinced

Photograph of full conditions taken by the author shortly after leaving the summit of Mount Lafayette.

retracing the way we had come would have been a better option. And going back alone may have been catastrophic. But the real point is that I didn't feel comfortable talking to these guys about my misgivings and our options.

So, we started our traverse of the ridgeline. Things didn't improve at that point; in fact, they got worse. Shortly after descending the slope of Lafayette and moving onto the ridge, we approached a sharp drop-off to our right—a drainage gully. As the westerly wind slammed into the slope below us, it caught the water, snow, and debris that usually run down the gully and catapulted them upward, onto, and over the ridgeline. It was, by far, the strongest wind I'd ever experienced, the proverbial freight train so often described by those who spend their time in alpine regions.

Greg was out front. As he approached the drainage, he stopped at the edge of the drop and turned to face the wind, extending his arms outward at shoulder length. Then he leaned forward over the edge, into the full force of the wind. Trusting the strength of the headwind to keep him from plummeting, headfirst, down the long, steep drop, he remained suspended, as Dave and I watched. When I reflect back on that moment, I don't consider what Greg did to be reckless or risky. The winds were certainly strong and steady enough to hold him up. What is clear to me, though, is how far apart Greg and I were in that place. We were feet from one another physically but galaxies away from one another emotionally. He was enthusiastically embracing the "full conditions," while I was retreating from them. Exhausted and fearful, I felt alone. At that moment, I was hiking solo, not willing to share my state of mind with the other two.

Moving along the ridge, we got pummeled from the side by the high winds and had to struggle to walk in a direct line. I grew increasingly fatigued. I hadn't hydrated or eaten and was at the point where you have expended nearly all your body's blood sugar through physical exertion. I was now in survival mode. My legs were cramping, and as the stiffness worked its way upward, I went to the one-foot-in-front-of-the-other contingency plan.

By this point my companions were out of sight, and I had to attempt to trace their footsteps in the snow before they were erased by the wind. I desperately searched for cairns to be sure I was staying squarely on the trail and not getting too close to the edge. Greg would occasionally emerge from the frozen fog, retracing his steps until we could see each other. No words were exchanged—just a brief glance—before he'd turn around and continue, but it was during those small moments of connection that I felt a sliver of safety. I have no idea whether he thought I was just tired or really in trouble, but with this small gesture, he was acknowledging and subtly managing my slow, halting progress.

After what seemed like an entire life span, we finally reached Little Haystack's summit, marking the end of the torturous ridge walk. Shortly thereafter we were back at tree line and, blessedly, out of the raging wind. I inhaled a PB&J sandwich and some hot chocolate, and immediately felt better. And at that moment, the day's story began to change.

That was awesome! I had just crossed an exposed ridge in winter and epic conditions! I was feeling euphoric even though, in reality, I was lucky to have survived the outing with only a badly bruised ego. Just a week later, in fact, two hikers from New Hampshire became trapped in a storm on the same ridgeline. One survived, but his companion perished.

My two hiking companions never spoke of my difficulties that day, and I have not hiked with them since. I'm not even sure they were aware of the degree of distress I was experiencing. We had shared a first date and then had never called each other again for a second one. Happens all the time, right?

A couple of days after the hike, I returned to the warmth and security of my office—where I work in risk management. That's right, my day job involves working with clients on how to manage their risk. And, yes, I am aware of the disconnect....

What did I take away from that day? Probably more questions than answers. But those questions will stay with me and, I hope, help me take better care of myself in high and low places. Can I master my ego enough to admit when I'm in over my head? Will I trust my hiking companions, my teammates, and my colleagues enough to share my concerns with them? Can I make myself stop, fuel up, and hydrate rather than carelessly pushing on? Can I forgo reaching my goals when it makes more sense to turn back while there's still time—and save the euphoria for another day? In the warmth of my flatland home, I can resolve to answer yes to every one of those questions. Back on the mountain? Well, we'll see.

This book is the story of another climber who faced "full conditions" in the extreme. I can know only part of Kate Matrosova's story, but what I do know has drawn me in and held me. A friend has told me he doesn't believe I found the story but that the story found me. Whatever the case, it has taught me much about aspiration, strength, and persistence and just as much about the importance of balancing those qualities with reflection, judgment, and restraint. There is a lot we can admire about Matrosova and much we can learn from her tragic end.

Franconia Ridge from Mount Lafayette.

I
INTERSECTION

"Her eyes were never bluer than when she was in the mountains."
—Charlie Farhoodi, husband of Kate Matrosova

Madison Col
Northern Presidential Range
White Mountain National Forest, New Hampshire
Sunday, Feb. 15, 2015
10:27 a.m.

Kate Matrosova is at an intersection. Later, it will be seen as both literal and figurative. She is alone at an elevation of 4,800 feet and standing in front of the locked, inaccessible Madison Spring Hut in what is known as the Madison Col. A col is the lowest point on a ridge that sits between two peaks, in this case, Mounts Madison and Adams.

Matrosova has just completed her first objective of the day: summiting the 5,366-foot Mount Madison. If she looks to her right at the Valley Way, her eyes watering from the robust north wind running through the col, she will spot the imprints created by her plastic mountaineering boots when she broke tree line toward Madison Hut an hour and a half earlier. While still discernable, her prints will soon be swept away by the constant winds.

For Matrosova, those footprints—which could lead her back down the Valley Way to the trailhead below—represent familiarity, safety, and comfort. But she has always embraced the unfamiliar and thrived on challenge, and she has developed a high tolerance for discomfort. At this moment, her goal lies four summits and some eleven hiking miles southward, where her planned 15-mile traverse of the Northern Presidential Range of the White Mountains should end later today.

The Mount Washington Regional Mesonet is a network of remote weather stations located throughout the White Mountains that continuously collect real-time weather data and transmit the information via solar-powered radio links to the Mount Washington Observatory website, where hikers can access it. There are no wind or temperature sensors in the Presidential Range north of Mount Washington, because the cost of installing one is prohibitive and, in any case, Mount Madison is out of the Observatory's sight line. The sensor closest to where Matrosova stands in the Madison Col is located at 5,300 feet on the Mount Washington Auto Road. The thermometer there shows a temperature of -10°F, which is very close to the air temperature she is experiencing. Unfortunately, ice and freezing temperatures render the sensor's anemometer (wind gauge) inoperable in winter, so we cannot know the exact wind speeds that are buffeting her, but we can look to the sensors on Mount Washington's summit for some indication.

Matrosova is standing eight trail miles north of Mount Washington's 6,288-foot summit, and she cannot know that sensors on that summit are showing signs of deteriorating weather. The temperature on the summit cone is -13°F with a windchill of -54°. Winds from the north are sustained at 50 mph, and gusting to 70. The winds and the cold are making their presence felt to the small number of Mount Washington Observatory and Mount Washington State Park staff members and volunteers occupying the summit buildings.

Yet below the summit, at 4,500 feet, the Cog Railway sensor, which sits at the cusp of tree line above the base of the Ammonoosuc Ravine Trail, where Matrosova's trip is meant to conclude later that day, tells a different story. At Cog, the winds glazing the western slope of Washington barely top 10 mph, gusting to no more than 20, and the temperature hovers just below zero. Variability is clearly the word of the day, not an unusual occurrence in these mountains and one that makes them difficult to read, especially for the uninitiated.

Matrosova knows nothing of this weather data. If she did, she might even feel encouraged by the report that the current weather at her intended finish line suggests she'll have a cakewalk by mountaineering standards. Though she has reached greater heights in mountains around the world, she is not experienced in this deceptively rugged and unpredictable range and so is unaware that the wild inconsistencies in temperature and wind recorded that day are reinforcing Mount Washington's reputation as the "Home of the World's Worst Weather."

Matrosova is certainly feeling the winds assailing her as she stands in the col. At midmorning on that Sunday, a sinister side of Mother Nature is gaining strength and approaching from the north. Its imminent arrival, heralded by the wind's deep, bellowing howls, has kept many White Mountain-savvy hikers at home or, at the very least, below tree line. Closer to the upper reaches of the atmosphere, Matrosova can see, hear, and feel the early stages of the forces at play, but she is relying on her instincts, which tell her the conditions will not reach full strength until later that day. As she ponders her next move, she is miscalculating how quickly the approaching front will bring with it dangers unfelt for many years—even in the harsh reality of these mountains.

If Matrosova looks to her left she will feel temporary relief from the wind that, like a shot of novocaine, begins with a sting and then brings on numbness. She will see the Star Lake Trail disappearing up and over a slight rise toward Mount Adams. But the low clouds enveloping the upper slopes of the range will be hiding the beautiful scenery that lies beyond the rise, and if she turns 360 degrees, she'll be unable to see the valleys below or the summits of the surrounding peaks.

She has chosen the Star Lake Trail to reach her second destination of the day: the summit of Mount Adams at 5,799 feet. Tracking southwest, the trail is a mile in length. Once it touches the eastern face of Adams, it rises 1,000 feet in a "steep and rough" ascent, as described in the Randolph Paths guidebook, before topping out at the summit.

A second option for reaching the summit of Adams is via the Gulfside and Air Line trails. That route is almost the same length as the Star Lake Trail, rising 1,000 feet to the summit and taking almost the same amount of time. While Star Lake provides protection from winds coming from the north/northwest, the Gulfside/Air Line route can serve as a better indicator of changes in wind direction and intensity. The Air Line's expansive ridgeline is fully exposed to the wind and can offer the hiker a clear idea of what to expect moving forward. But though the latter option might offer more information, it is understandable that Matrosova decides to stick to her original plan, which will slightly shield her from the impact of the current conditions even as it prevents her from recognizing the signs of worsening weather ahead.

Matrosova's legs have likely recharged by now after her fifty-minute descent of Madison, though she has not been able to enter Madison Spring Hut for warmth because it is locked and boarded up in winter. She reaches into her pack and retrieves a GoPro camera mounted on a homemade selfie-stick that her husband, Charlie Farhoodi, made for her the day before. They couldn't find a real one in any of the local stores, so he rigged one up with a plastic dowel and some packing tape. It isn't pretty, but it works, and it brings Charlie close at that moment. Matrosova extends the selfie-stick away from her with her gloved right hand, tucks her right elbow into her midsection, steadies the camera with her left hand to hold the gusting winds at bay, and takes two photographs of herself. She places the camera back in her pack, secures the flap, and slings the forty-five-liter pack over her shoulders. It's cold; it's later than she would like; and it's time to move.

The choice she will make right then—between turning right onto the Valley Way and descending the way she came or turning left onto the Star Lake Trail, as planned, and making her way toward Mount Adams—will cost Matrosova her life in approximately five hours.

II
CONVERGENCE

"The laws of celestial mechanics dictate that when two objects collide, there is always damage, of a collateral nature."
    —*Professor Moriarty to Sherlock Holmes*

Weather instrument tower, summit of Mount Washington, in favorable winter conditions. The Northern Presidentials are in the background.

Mount Washington Observatory
Sargent's Purchase, Coos County, N.H.
Wednesday, Feb. 11, 2015
5:56 a.m.

Tom Padham is sitting at his workstation in a building on the summit of the Northeast's highest peak. As a staff meteorologist for the Mount Washington Observatory, he is in the process of posting online that day's first *Mount Washington Observatory Weather Forecast*. The observatory posts two such forecasts each day, one early in the morning and another in the evening. Part of this report includes two "Forecast Discussions," one for the "Higher Summits" and another for "Mount Washington Valley." The Higher Summits forecast covers the entire 23-mile Presidential Range and the many surrounding peaks. It provides those who plan to visit higher elevations, either by chairlift or hiking boot, a sense of what is to come, especially on weekends when thousands flock to the region to recreate.

If Observatory staff members see something significant on the weather horizon for an upcoming weekend, they will start a discussion in their forecasts as early as Wednesday. Today is one of those days. Just before 6 a.m., Padham will post the following:

> High pressure will crest over New England today, with a clipper system approaching from the west this evening. Clouds will begin to increase this afternoon ahead of low pressure, with temperatures above average today in the teens. Overnight skies will become mostly cloudy, with a few snow showers possible shortly before dawn. Low pressure will redevelop south of New England late tomorrow before rapidly intensifying, with the storm staying far enough offshore to only keep a few snow showers in the forecast into Friday morning. Much colder air will move in behind this storm, with temperatures looking to remain well below zero across the higher summits through the weekend.

A little over twelve hours later, Padham's colleague, intern Nate Iannuccillo, will post that evening's forecast. While largely consistent with Padham's, Iannuccillo's Higher Summits forecast strikes a meteorological alarm in its final two sentences:

> Friday will see partial clearing throughout the day as high pressure builds in the wake of the front's passage. Temperatures will stay cold throughout the day as arctic air moves in from northwest Canada.

The pieces on the Presidential Range's weather chessboard are starting to move. On Thursday, Feb. 12, the evening post will include a winter storm watch in effect from Saturday afternoon through Sunday night. A "watch" indicates that storm conditions are expected but not yet imminent.

Manhattan, New York City
Friday, Feb. 13, 2015
Sometime after 5:00 p.m.

In the apartment Kate Matrosova and her husband, Charlie Farhoodi, moved into the previous fall, Matrosova is addressing last-minute preparations for the six-hour drive they will make in a rental car the following morning to northern New Hampshire, some 370 miles away.

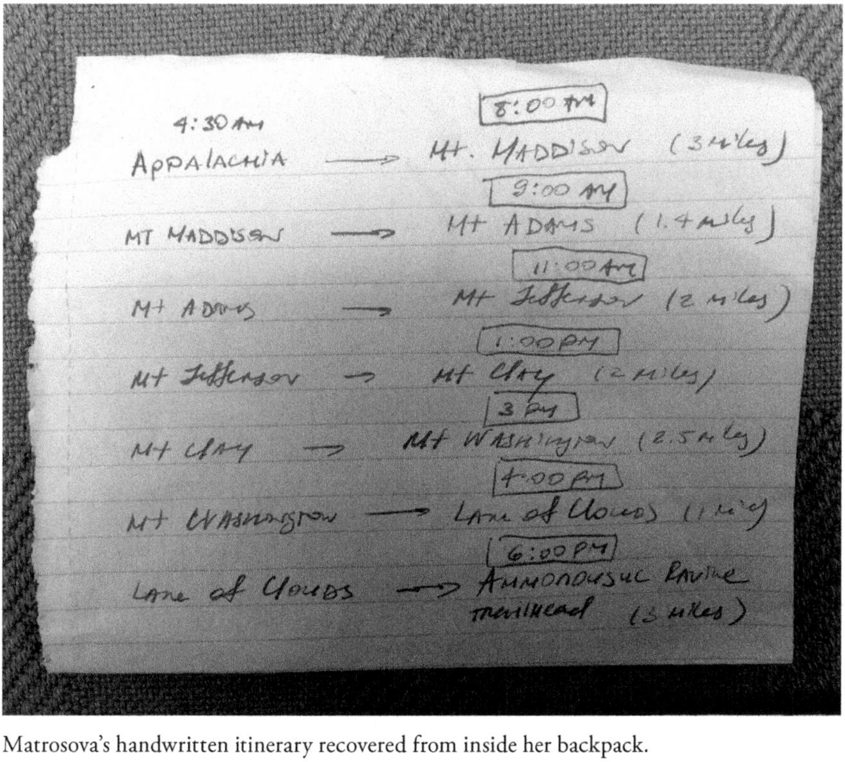

Matrosova's handwritten itinerary recovered from inside her backpack.

Matrosova works in credit derivatives for Banque Nationale de Paris (BNP Paribas), and Farhoodi is a vice president for J.P. Morgan Chase. Both banks are massive, both jobs demanding. They feel it will do them good to escape the high-pressure world of investment banking for a few days, as Matrosova points toward a Northern Presidential Traverse in the White Mountains on Sunday.

Shortly after Matrosova arrives home, she readies her gear for the long journey northward. Earlier that day, the Mount Washington Observatory Weather Forecast again showed a winter storm watch for Saturday afternoon through Sunday evening, but the evening forecast, posted at 6:18 p.m., has upgraded the watch to a warning, indicating that forecasted conditions are already occurring or are imminent. On Sunday, winds from the north on the higher summits are expected to be between 80 and 100 mph, with gusts to 115. Windchill temperatures are expected to drop to between -60°F and -70°F.

We don't know if Matrosova checks the worsening forecast before the two begin to make their way north. If she does, it might not cause her to abandon her weekend's hiking goal, which she has outlined in a handwritten itinerary housed in the top compartment of her backpack. Her hike is still two days out and, she might think, the forecast could always change for the better.

Holiday Inn Express
Lincoln, N.H.
Saturday, Feb. 14, 2015
8:00 a.m.

Forty-eight miles south of where Matrosova and Farhoodi will be staying for the weekend, Erik Thatcher is also spending his morning at a hotel. Thatcher is a guide for Mooney Mountain Guides, and the director of the Climbing Program at Holderness School, a small independent school about twenty minutes to the south of the hotel where Thatcher is now co-leading a winter hiking course.

Thanks to his parents' love of the outdoors, Thatcher enjoyed an active childhood and became skilled at hiking, paddling, and biking. In high school, he took up rock and ice climbing and spent extensive time climbing out West. Mentored by seasoned climbers and guides, he became highly competent, earning certifications in wilderness medicine, avalanche safety, and technical climbing. In addition to teaching and guiding, which he has done since 2011, Thatcher is a member of the Androscoggin Valley Search and Rescue (AVSAR) team, a small volunteer organization of hikers and climbers who respond to outdoor emergencies throughout the North Country. He is also part of AVSAR's Winter Above Tree Line Team, an even smaller group of highly experienced mountain experts who go above tree line in winter to conduct searches and rescues.

On this winter day, Thatcher is new to the AVSAR team and has yet to participate in his first emergency call. He has no idea that, very soon, he will be called upon to do so. For now, it is day one of the two-day winter mountaineering course offered by Recreational Equipment Inc. (REI), and Thatcher and his fellow instructor, Alex Teixeira, are imparting some of their vast alpine knowledge to their seven participants, teaching them the basics of winter hiking. They cover topics ranging from proper hiking gear, hydration and food choices, self-care, self-rescue, and effective layering of winter clothing.

They'll place a lot of emphasis on layering over the next two days, because regulating body temperature in cold weather is critical to success and survival. The proper system begins with a wicking layer closest to the body to remove perspiration away from the skin and out through the other layers. A mid-layer piece comes next, adding insulating warmth, and a shell layer goes on over it as a barrier to keep rain and snow away from the inner layers. As you heat up or cool off, and as weather conditions change, you remove or add layers to keep yourself protected and your body temperature stable.

After demonstrating such layering and the proper method of loading gear into a backpack, the instructors spend time with each participant assessing the gear they've brought to the session. If something is missing, or not appropriate for winter hiking, they'll either lend them their own gear or recommend one of the many gear shops in Lincoln where the proper equipment can be found. At 10:00 a.m., after organizing themselves and their gear, the group drives twenty minutes south for the next phase of instruction, a winter hike above tree line on the Welch and Dickey Loop Trail. For some in the group, today's climb will serve as the warm-up for a planned ascent of Mount Washington the following day.

The Bunkhouse at Northeast Mountaineering
Glen, N.H.
Saturday, Feb. 14, 2015
9:00 a.m.

Like his fellow guide Erik Thatcher to the south, Corey Fitzgerald is in instruction mode. Along with his younger brother Brett, he is a co-owner of the New Hampshire-based guiding company Northeast Mountaineering. Fitzgerald also fell in love with the outdoors at a young age and first hiked in the White Mountains when he was eight years old. Over the past several years, he has acquired extensive alpine knowledge, summiting Denali in Alaska; several peaks in Washington State, including Rainier; and a number of peaks in South America. Also deeply experienced in the Whites, Fitzgerald has summited Mount Washington more than forty times, completed the entire Presidential Traverse seven times in winter, and done a number of winter loops on Madison and Adams, much of this while guiding clients. Along the way, he has earned certifications in avalanche safety and technical climbing instruction and is a certified Wilderness Emergency Medical Technician (WEMT). Like Thatcher, Fitzgerald is a new member of AVSAR and also a pending member of the Winter Above Tree Line Team but has yet to participate in an emergency call. And as it will for Thatcher, that is about to change.

On this day, Fitzgerald is standing in the common area of the company-owned Bunkhouse, providing instruction to two budding mountaineers very similar to that being offered by Thatcher and Teixeira. After gear rentals and checks, the three leave the Bunkhouse and head about twenty minutes south and west to Crawford Notch, where they'll also learn and practice winter hiking skills. And just like three of Thatcher's students, they will be on the slopes of Mount Washington tomorrow.

Thatcher, Teixeira, and Fitzgerald, and other instructors and guides throughout the region, continuously stress the importance of self-care, especially in winter. Hydration and nutrition are critical to maintaining our energy and body warmth, and we must be mindful of the way each safety technique works with all the others. To maintain our body's core temperature of 98.6°F, we must balance heat production, heat conservation, and heat loss, a practice known as thermoregulation. As the core temperature of our body drops, we get cold and start to shiver, which is our body's attempt to generate warmth. Shivering increases the body's expenditure of oxygen, which we use to burn calories, so when we are exceedingly cold, it becomes difficult to take in and burn enough calories to keep ourselves sufficiently fueled. As we get colder, we start to experience a slight degree of cognitive impairment, which can prevent us from making sound decisions about self-care. Once we become fatigued by cold and lack of fuel, "self-care is the first thing to go," explains Fitzgerald. Which is why it's important to begin self-care from the start, before anything begins to go wrong.

Stonehearth Open Learning Opportunities (SOLO) of Conway, N.H., the oldest continuously operating school of wilderness medicine in the world, offers a great primer on self-care. It's called *Wildcare*, and its purpose is to instruct wilderness medicine practitioners and those of us who like to venture out and sometimes find ourselves "working in less than desirable conditions and remote environments." *Wildcare* stresses that our survival in harsh conditions depends on "the conscious, voluntary set of actions that we take to protect ourselves."

One of the ways we get into trouble, according to *Wildcare*, is by not doing what we should to counteract heat loss during winter hikes. Hikers in winter can lose heat and gain cold in numerous ways. Touching metal with bare skin or poorly insulated gloves, for example, can lead to rapid heat loss through conduction. As a hiker perspires during exertion in cold weather, the heat of his body is carried away by the windchill and replaced by the surrounding, cooler air, lowering his body temperature. Perspiration also evaporates into the cooler air, adding to heat loss and the need for hydration. All this points to the necessity for proper clothing, consistent hydration, and good nutrition. That is why Fitzgerald and Thatcher spend so much time checking their students' and clients' supplies, gear, and clothing, and teaching self-care skills before taking them out to hike or climb.

For Thatcher and Fitzgerald, safety trumps peak-bagging every time. They are acutely aware of how cold and windy it's going to be the next day on Mount Washington as they make their way up the slopes. Not only will they need to monitor and manage their clients' safety, they'll need to do the same for themselves. They'll need to keep themselves and their clients hydrated, fed, and warm, and watch carefully for early signs of hypothermia.

Mount Washington Auto Road
Saturday, Feb. 14, 2015
9:45 a.m.

Ryan Knapp is riding in the protective cab of a snowcat, a burly vehicle the size of a box truck, with full tracks. The "cat" resembles a military tank without the gun turret. It serves as an alpine shuttle for people and supplies heading to and from the buildings that stand atop Mount Washington. The State of New Hampshire operates Mount Washington State Park and leases space to the Mount Washington

Observatory, where Knapp has worked since 2005 as the senior staff meteorologist and weather observer.

Today, Knapp is behind schedule. In fact, he's a day late for work. But his tardiness is excused because it is understandable. After a few extra days off, he was supposed to be at his desk the previous day, but Mother Nature forced the snowcat he was riding in to turn around at 4,000 feet. "If the operator of the snowcat can't see beyond the plow blade, we turn around," Knapp explains. The retreat had been a wise move. There was dense fog, limiting visibility on the mountain to one-eighth of a mile. Winds were averaging 50 mph, and at one point that day, there was a gust of 89 mph. If Knapp and his companion had been required to get off the snowcat, they would have encountered a windchill that had lowered the temperature to -57°F, ready to wreak havoc on any exposed skin.

Today, though, Mother Nature has loosened her grip. On his ride up the Auto Road, Knapp is enjoying a view of 90 miles, winds are in the mid-30s, and it is a bit warmer at -12°F. For a novice rider, the ninety-minute trip (on a good day) can be intimidating. At different points on the road in winter, operators are forced to drop the snowcat's blade and plow through the snowdrifts that pile up on the 7.6-mile route. Leaving the drifts unplowed would make the Auto Road completely impassable. There are no guardrails anywhere on the route, so inexperienced passengers often find themselves sliding toward the driver's side of the seat thinking the weight shift will prevent the snowcat from toppling down a steep slope or over a hairpin turn and into the base of Great Gulf, thousands of feet below.

But Knapp, an old hand, is unfazed by the precarious feel of the ascent and eager to work his normal 5:30 p.m. to 5:30 a.m. shifts over the next several days. A summit meteorologist works Wednesday to Wednesday before descending to the valley below for a well-deserved break.

Knapp and his colleagues have been texting one another for days. "All of us were watching the weather," Knapp says. On the summit of Mount Washington, he and his colleagues have the best seats in the house, positioned at the dead center of three converging storm tracks. Approaching storms come from three directions: up the Atlantic Ocean, where nor'easters and hurricanes are fueled; up the Ohio River Valley to the Saint Lawrence River Valley; and across the Great Lakes and up the Saint Lawrence River Valley. The fronts build from the evaporating water they travel over.

"If it forms anywhere in the lower forty-eight, it will most likely hit the Northeast," says Knapp. "Everything will funnel its way through here." With weather moving west to east or southwest to northeast, Mount Washington sits at the intersection of these tracks and so bears the brunt of converging paths. There's nothing else high enough to slow or weaken the storms before they arrive.

Once at the summit, Knapp retrieves his gear, helps load and unload a "fire line" of bags sitting just outside the main building, checks in with his colleagues, and then heads to bed to get some sleep before the start of his shift later that afternoon.

Royalty Inn
Gorham, N.H.
Saturday, Feb. 14, 2015

Sometime after 3:00 p.m., Matrosova and Farhoodi's rental car pulls into the parking lot of the Royalty Inn on Main Street in Gorham, N.H. Today is Valentine's Day and for them the start of the long Presidents Day weekend. The region is familiar to them. They have been here once before, a month ago in fact, for a reconnaissance visit.

Like others anticipating a hike in the Presidentials the following day, Matrosova will soon complete final preparations for her planned traverse. It's common for hikers and climbers to lay out their gear for a visual inventory before systematically loading it into their backpacks. Here is what Matrosova will carry in her High Sierra Summit 45 pack:

Smith goggles

Two Apple iPhones (one phone, one music w/headphones)

Garmin Global Positioning System (GPS), model 62s

Suunto Vector wristwatch

Appalachian Mountain Club (AMC) White Mountain Trail Map 29th Edition (route black-lined)

Handwritten hiking itinerary w/pen

Nivea chapstick

Inmarsat Satellite Phone w/case

ACR ResQLink 375 Personal Locator Beacon (PLB)

GoPro Hero3 Camera taped to 15-inch plastic dowel rod

Ziploc bag of food (apple, tangerine, granola bars, peanuts, fruit snacks, and Quaker Popped Rice crisps)

Bose zipped case with GoPro battery and camera remote activator

Blue Nalgene 32-ounce water bottle (full)

White Nalgene 32-ounce water bottle (full) in blue neoprene holder

Red Nalgene 32-ounce water bottle (full) in blue neoprene holder

LED headlamp

Smith bag (for goggles)

Black Diamond crampons w/case

Foster Grant sunglasses w/case

Yalumi LED light

Journal with blue paper cover

Just as Thatcher and Fitzgerald's students are being taught to use their clothing as a layering system, Matrosova will pack and dress in a way that shows she plans to do exactly that:

Pair of black North Face gloves

Outdoor Research Primaloft gloves

Outdoor Research glove liners

Pair of black Columbia mitts

Green winter hat

Burton black winter hat

Mountain Hardware down pants

REI spandex/nylon pants

North Face Flight Series pants

Marmot down jacket

Patagonia hooded jacket

Under Armour Inner jacket

Marmot Gore-Tex hooded shell

Marmot outer shell pants

REI gaiters

Wool socks

La Sportiva mountaineering boots

She is also reported to have taken trekking poles, a thermos of hot tea, and a mountaineering ax, but those items were never recovered.

Welch and Dickey trailhead parking lot, Thornton, N.H.
Wiley's Slide parking area, Crawford Notch, N.H.
Saturday, Feb. 14, 2015
3:00 p.m.

Erik Thatcher and Alex Teixeira, and Corey Fitzgerald nearby, are summarizing the day's activities for the groups they are guiding. Thatcher and Teixeira have just led their group through the 4.1-mile loop trail, summiting Mounts Welch and Dickey along the way. On the steeper terrain, they donned crampons and learned to walk cautiously and maximize traction. With several rock slabs along the route, Thatcher and Teixeira regularly asked them to drop their packs and walk circuits up and down the ice and snow-covered rock to build their confidence walking on crampons.

They also instructed their students on the proper method of self-arrest, allowing them to practice on the gentler slopes of the route. If a hiker is ascending steep terrain hard-packed with snow or ice, he or she is generally wearing crampons or micro-spikes and holding a mountaineering ax attached to a leash and secured to the hiker's wrist. In the event the hiker falls, she rolls onto her stomach and, keeping the ax to the side with the pick down, drives her weight onto the top of the adze end of the ax in order to create friction and stop. The hiker must be careful to keep her boots in the air so as not to catch a crampon spike in the snow and spin around, perhaps sliding headfirst or seriously injuring her leg. While Thatcher himself has become expert in self-arrest techniques in an instructional environment, he has not yet needed to use them, for which he feels lucky.

Corey Fitzgerald's afternoon has been similar. He has introduced his two students to Wiley's Slide, a large and relatively low-angled ice slab that provides ample opportunity for mountaineers to practice ice anchors, rope belays, and climbing techniques. But today, Fitzgerald has decided to stick to the same methodical basics that Thatcher and Teixeira focused on, since his students are not yet ready for more advanced training.

By midafternoon, students from both courses are tired after a long day of instruction. Those intending to return the following day will need extra time to rest and acquire any additional gear they might need before engaging Mount Washington. In their respective parking lots, the instructors take the opportunity to communicate expectations to each of their groups. They mention the daunting weather forecast before cutting students loose for the rest of the day. Given what is expected, a good night's sleep will likely prove valuable—if they can manage it.

Thatcher, Teixeira, and their clients descending Mount Dickey on Feb. 14, 2015.

Climbers on Wiley's Slide in Crawford Notch, where Fitzgerald instructed his two clients.

Mount Washington Observatory
Saturday, Feb. 14, 2015
5:30 p.m.

After waking at 2:00 p.m., Ryan Knapp prepares himself for that night's shift. During the afternoon briefing, held at 4:00 p.m., he and his colleagues discuss the day shift's observations, the current and forecasted weather, and optimum timing for snowcat runs.

An area of low pressure has approached the region during the day, which has allowed a warm front to move northward. As the low has approached, winds throughout the day have averaged a moderate 25–40 mph. The temperature has warmed since sunrise, from -10° F to -5°F, and is expected to continue to warm overnight as Knapp works his shift. The low-pressure area will pass over the region around midnight, winds atop Mount Washington will bottom out at 10 mph, and the temperature will rise to about 0°F.

As the low-pressure area moves away and into the Gulf of Maine, it will rapidly intensify over the Atlantic Ocean. This strengthening of the warmer low-pressure area combined with the colder high-pressure area moving in behind it from the west (the approaching polar air mass from Northwest Canada) will cause a weather phenomenon known as bombogenesis, which meteorologists refer to more informally as a "weather bomb" or "bombing out." Bombogenesis occurs when there is a steep drop in air pressure and a significant temperature gradiant between a cold continental air mass and a warmer air mass over the ocean. The forecast calls for bombogenesis to drive up wind speeds, and the models are showing that the extreme cold and high winds will soon converge on the Northern Presidentials.

Though Mount Washington Observatory denizens see gusts exceeding 100 mph nine or ten times a month, they experience what they consider "really big winds" much less frequently. Tomorrow, they won't see the 231-mph gust of 1934, but there is the potential for a repeat of the 145-mph winds recorded in 2008. For Knapp, such a possibility is exciting to anticipate, but he has work to do before he will know if it will materialize.

Royalty Inn
Gorham, N.H.
Saturday, Feb. 14, 2015
Evening

Kate Matrosova visits the Mount Washington Observatory website and checks the weather forecast for the next day. She is seeing the same report, posted at 5:10 p.m., that Knapp has consulted: "In the clouds with snow in the morning. Temperature dropping to 20 below in the afternoon. Winds from the east shifting north at 80-100 mph with gusts up to 125 mph. Windchill 55-65 below zero."

She may have also noted the following caveat, which accompanies all the Observatory's weather postings: "Mountain weather is subject to rapid changes and extreme conditions. This outlook is just one tool to help you plan a safe trip. Always travel with adequate clothing, shelter, food, and water, and make your own assessment of weather conditions."

As it turns out, that is the last weather forecast Matrosova will check before departing the next morning on what she intends to be a fast traverse that will get her down before the predicted storm hits and at a speed that will keep her warm enough to ward off the cold.

...wing snow on summit of Mount Clay.

III
THE PLAN

"Apply your ambition with knowledge."
—*Kelly Cordes, climber and author of* The Tower

Royalty Inn
Gorham, N.H.
Sunday, Feb. 15, 2015
Shortly before 5:00 a.m.

Matrosova has planned to start her day very early. Given her itinerary—15 miles and five summits—an early rise is absolutely essential. At 4:30 a.m., when she plans to reach the trailhead, it will be more than two hours before dawn reaches the eastern slopes of the Northern Presidential Range she plans to traverse, though the sun will not be there to meet her today. Unfortunately, however, Matrosova and Farhoodi sleep past their early alarm. That delay will steal thirty minutes of precious time from Matrosova's carefully plotted itinerary, and she will not arrive at the trailhead until 5:00 a.m.

The couple moves quickly around the small hotel room, making sure to collect all her gear and supplies. In her hurry to catch up with her schedule, Matrosova doesn't log in to the Mount Washington Observatory's website. Even if she were to check, the early reading might not deter her, since she is confident she can beat the impending storm front.

As the two leave their room with Matrosova's gear in tow, she is likely trying hard to muffle the clunking sounds of her stiff plastic mountaineering boots for fear of waking sleeping guests of the hotel at this hour. Emerging outside into the crisp morning air, they will immediately see their breath as they walk across the well-lit parking lot to the car. Both will likely have noted easy, 10-mph winds, no gusts, and a temperature of 6°F, as detected by one of the mesonet weather sensors located right next door in Berlin. The car motor, the scraping of ice from the windshield, and the hum of the parking lot lights overhead are likely the only sounds audible in this pleasant community of 2,848 sleeping residents. At that early hour on a Sunday morning, especially in winter, it is unlikely they will encounter any other vehicles on the road during their 6.4-mile drive to the Appalachia parking lot on Route 2 in Randolph. Appalachia, managed by the Appalachian Mountain Club (AMC) and the launch pad for several trails leading to the northern peaks of the Presidentials, is where Matrosova will set in motion her finely tuned itinerary. Her plan is to complete the 15-mile northern chunk of the 23-mile full traverse in a single day, in a "light and fast manner." And she will do it solo.

Rick Wilcox, owner of International Mountain Equipment in Conway, N.H., and an accomplished mountaineer and volunteer rescuer, will later explain to a reporter from the *Conway Daily Sun*, "There are two ways to go: light and fast, or heavy and slow. If something happens when you go light and fast, you're screwed, because [without the necessary gear] there is no way to spend the night. If you're on Lion Head on Mount Washington, and there are forty or fifty people around and you get into trouble, that's one thing. If you're in the Northern Presidentials and you get into trouble, there is no one to help you."

In opting for the light-and-fast mode, Matrosova has chosen to complete the traverse with the minimal amount of gear necessary in order to move through the terrain quickly. Speed often equals safety, because the less time you are out in an unstable weather system or risky environment, the less exposed you are to its dangers. This is what she is counting on as she sets off.

The downside to the light-and-fast method is that you are carrying very little emergency gear that can help you ride out a storm or await help following an injury. Yet, the heavy-and-slow method Wilcox describes also has its downside. The slower you move through an unstable environment, the longer you will remain exposed. But as Wilcox aptly explains, at least you will have the necessary gear to provide shelter and warmth in an emergency.

Known as a supremely confident and planful person, the five-feet-seven-inch, 125-pound Matrosova believes that her high level of physical fitness and her lighter cache of gear will allow her to move across the fully exposed ridgelines in time to beat the early weather forecast she has seen. She expects to be at the southern end of her itinerary and approaching the safety of tree line on the Ammonoosuc Ravine Trail by the time the forecasted winds are to arrive. She knows it will be cold, so she plans to keep moving because she does not want to be on the trail, especially above tree line, after dark. With darkness comes limited visibility, and since Matrosova has never done this traverse, she doesn't want to put herself at undue risk. In fact, to ensure that she will be in safe territory before dark, she chooses not to bring the added weight of snowshoes or a shelter (tent, bivy sack, or sleeping bag).

The idea to do the Northern Traverse was born during a wilderness navigation course that Matrosova and Farhoodi once took together in upstate New York. Their guide suggested they consider the traverse, and that conversation sowed the seed in Matrosova's mind. She and Farhoodi discussed the possibility of his accompanying her on the traverse, but they agreed she'd be moving at a pace that would be unsustainable for him. She then tried to recruit people from their hiking circle to go along, but none would bite. One of her hiking companions even questioned her wish to do the traverse, suggesting that it wasn't worth the effort and that she should seek bigger challenges. But Matrosova was determined, and her friend realized that once she had set her mind on something, there would be no dissuading her.

Matrosova was admired by co-workers and hiking companions for her off-the-charts optimism and goal-orientated nature. Everything she did was well planned. When faced with a difficult challenge, she would try her best to bend the activity to her will— and, from all reports, most of the time it *would* bend.

Companions say that, for Matrosova, the mountains were about engaging in a spiritual connection with nature as well as about enjoying a good challenge. She viewed the Northern Presidential Traverse as a chance to do both. So when a fellow hiker questioned the achievement value of completing the traverse—a potentially risky venture depending on weather, but not a big-ticket item for anyone hoping to become a world-class mountaineer—it did not deter Matrosova, because she was interested in her own sense of connection and achievement, not in anyone else's opinion of its value.

After her unsuccessful attempt to recruit companions for the traverse, Matrosova began the process of developing her solo plan. She had a great deal of information at her disposal, both online and in excellently written guidebooks. But she was not familiar with the White Mountains and so did not have the wisdom that can be acquired by talking with local mountain guides and becoming acclimated to the rugged terrain and weather. Still, she used the information she had to shape the logistics of her hike, recording them in notepads and on maps. She compiled and tested the gear she would need and maintained her high level of fitness as she looked ahead to the adventure.

Her completed plan relies on timing and speed, and though she doesn't bring snowshoes to navigate potentially deep snows, she does include safety contingencies. She identifies six potential bailout points at various locations along the route. Bailout points serve as refuges in the event a hiker needs to retreat because of time constraints, weather, injury, or some combination of the three. According to Matrosova's handwritten itinerary, Farhoodi will drop her off at the Appalachia trailhead at 4:30 a.m. She will take the 3.8-mile Valley Way, ascending a total of 3,500 feet to the AMC's Madison Spring Hut. Sunrise that morning will be at 6:44 a.m., so she will be navigating the early stages of the trail by headlamp. From Madison Spring Hut at 4,800 feet, she will climb Mount Madison (5,366 feet), arriving at the summit by 8:00 a.m.

Matrosova's itinerary allots less time than the guidebooks do to move from one summit to the next, but this is not unusual, since guidebook times tend to be conservative, and Matrosova is highly fit and would certainly count on soundly beating those times.

From Madison Spring Hut, she plans to turn left onto Star Lake Trail and, with the lower satellite peak of John Quincy Adams (5,410 feet) to her right, hike one mile to the summit of Mount Adams (at 5,799 feet, the second highest peak in New Hampshire) by 9:00 a.m.

She will then descend Adams and approach Thunderstorm Junction, where Gulfside Trail, Great Gully Trail, and Lowes Path converge. It is here that Matrosova can access her first bailout point, if needed. Lowes Path takes a hiker over another satellite peak (Abigail Adams, at 5,355 feet) to Gray Knob Cabin, owned and operated by the Randolph Mountain Club. Gray Knob is open year-round and has a caretaker on-site 24/7. A hiker can find heat and shelter there. A handwritten notation on her black-lined map of the route indicates that Matrosova believes it will take her fifty minutes to walk from Thunderstorm Junction to Gray Knob cabin, if she needs to bail out. This is not an unrealistic calculation if a hiker has the skill to navigate the snow conditions, wind strength and direction, and low visibility.

If all goes well, however, Matrosova will link up with the Gulfside Trail and, keeping Mount Sam Adams (5,585 feet) to her right, approach the Israel Ridge Path also to her right, which will lead to her second bailout point, if she were to need it. The Perch, a three-sided wooden shelter above Israel Ridge, isn't an ideal shelter in bad conditions, but it provides some protection from the elements for a distressed hiker. From The Perch, Matrosova can also link up with Gray Knob Trail and continue on to Gray Knob Cabin.

If she doesn't require a bailout at this point, either, Matrosova will continue on the Gulfside and across Edmands Col, another glacially created carve-out and natural funnel for winds. From the col, she plans to ascend and summit Mount Jefferson (5,705 feet) by 11:00 a.m.

She has noted, however, that she can still bail out from Edmands Col if she needs to, linking up with the Israel Ridge Trail and working her way back north to The Perch and/or Gray Knob Cabin.

Descending Jefferson via the short Jefferson Loop Trail, she will link back up with the Gulfside. Just beyond Sphinx Dome and through Sphinx Col she will approach her fourth bailout point, which involves a left-hand turn onto Sphinx Trail. This is a desperation bailout point. It is meant to get the hiker below tree line as soon as possible, allowing her to dig a snow cave and ride out the tempest above. Matrosova has calculated it will take her fifteen minutes to get from the Gulfside Trail to below tree line on the Sphinx Trail, if need be.

Assuming a bailout is again not required, Matrosova will continue on the Gulfside Trail and take the Clay Loop Trail. After a two-mile hike from Jefferson, she will arrive at the summit of Mount Clay (5,533 feet) by 1:00 p.m. Descending from Clay and remaining on the loop trail into Clay Col, Matrosova will link back up with the Gulfside Trail and reach the intersection leading to her fifth bailout point. Turning right and walking back north on Gulfside, she can turn left onto the Jewell Trail and down to tree line and the Base Road, where the Cog Railway is located. She calculates that it will take her twenty-five minutes to get from Gulfside to tree line.

But if nothing untoward occurs, Matrosova will stay on the Gulfside Trail and head toward her final and highest peak of the day, Mount Washington (6,288 feet). She will still have one bailout point

left in case of emergency: the Cog Railway tracks. The tracks are known in wilderness navigation parlance as a "catching feature," a place that a lost or injured hiker will recognize. She calculates that it will take her one hour and twenty-five minutes along the railroad tracks to get from tree line to the Cog Railway Station, if she needs to bail out at this late stage of the traverse.

Despite these contingency plans, Matrosova assumes all will go smoothly and that she will reach Washington's summit by 3:00 p.m. She will then descend a mile via the Crawford Path, arriving at AMC's Lakes of the Clouds Hut (5,012 feet and, like Madison Spring Hut, locked in winter) at 4:00 p.m. From the hut she will descend via the Ammonoosuc Ravine Trail, reaching tree line just before sunset at 5:17 p.m. With her headlamp to light the way, she will descend the final three miles and meet Farhoodi at the Ammonoosuc Ravine trailhead at 6:00 p.m.

So that is the plan. And if conditions on the route are optimal, it is achievable. But if you ask local guides and seasoned White Mountain hikers, they will tell you that "optimal" conditions on the Northern Traverse in winter are still not ideal. Because Matrosova is traveling so light and relying on speed alone, the margin for error in her plan is thin. For her to succeed, everything will have to go right. For her to stay safe, she will have to be vigilant about self-care from the start and be able to reach one of her bailout points in case of distress. All of these, as it happens, lie beyond the summit of Mount Adams.

In establishing bailout points and packing cell and satellite phones, a GPS device, a map, and a personal locator beacon, Matrosova is acknowledging the existence of risk on the traverse. She has established a risk management plan. But given her inexperience in the White Mountains, is her plan comprehensive enough to address the multitude of exposures that exist there, especially in winter?

In their book *Risk Assessment*, Etti Baranoff, Scott Harrington, and Gregory Niehaus identify six steps that lead to an effective risk management plan. Their six-step process can work on a ridgeline, at home, or in the workplace. Here is what they suggest:

1. Identify your loss exposures (your risk of failure and loss)

2. Analyze your loss exposures (how critical is the failure or loss?)

3. Examine the feasibility of various risk management techniques

4. Select the appropriate risk management techniques

5. Implement the selected risk management techniques

6. Monitor results and revise the risk management program as you go along

A loss exposure is defined as "any condition that presents a possibility of loss, whether or not an actual loss occurs." In Matrosova's case, this exposure involves anything, known or unknown, that will interfere with her ability to achieve her goal of completing the traverse. She might have to contend with unpredictable or difficult terrain; adverse weather conditions; time pressure; inadequate, malfunctioning, or missing equipment; or factors that will affect her ability to function at optimum level, such as injury, extreme fatigue, or emotional distress.

To address the risks she is able to identify, Matrosova should use the information and data at her disposal to answer as many questions as she can before setting out. A meticulous researcher and planner, she will study guidebooks and craft a detailed plan that includes contingencies. But will she understand the wild unpredictability of winter weather in the White Mountains and the dangerous effects extreme weather will have on the rugged terrain with which she is unfamiliar? Should she pay closer attention to the early weather forecasts from the Mount Washington Observatory and plan to check for updates more frequently, including when she is on the trail?

Risk control is defined, in part, as "a conscious act or decision not to act that reduces the frequency and severity of losses." In other words, to control risk, you need to avoid and prevent exposure by making the right decisions at the right time. Having identified her potential exposures, are there any Matrosova can avoid or prevent? Is her plan to travel light and fast a good way to avoid the risk presented by an impending storm?

To decide on the best risk management techniques to employ, Matrosova should calculate the costs and benefits of each. If she chooses to add gear, and thus weight, based on weather predictions, will that cost her time and compromise her ability to complete the traverse before dark? But will the extra gear have the benefit of additional safety if she is caught out after dark? She clearly opts to avoid being slowed down, perhaps a natural response from someone used to meeting challenges and outrunning danger.

Matrosova's risk management plan is only as good as her ability to implement it. Does she have enough training with her equipment in similar conditions? What aspects of her personality and behavior must she understand—and be able to manage—as she reaches decision points?

Once she has embarked on her hike, with her risk assessment and management plan in place, Matrosova will need to maintain a high level of awareness in order to monitor changes in conditions and the emergence of new risks. Given the instability and unpredictability of the environment she is in, she will have to be willing to revise her plan and adapt to changes if she hopes to succeed and stay safe.

A key to all this is timing. Even with a well-developed risk management strategy and the ability to implement it effectively, Matrosova will have to decide if and when to trigger alterations to her original plan. In the end, it will be the timing of her decisions that will make all the difference.

IV
RISING

"He or she who is willing to be the most uncomfortable is not only the bravest but rises the fastest."
—Dr. Brené Brown, University of Houston

Appalachia Parking Lot
Route 2, Randolph, N.H.
Feb. 15, 2015
5:00 a.m.

To the uninterested or distracted passersby, the parking lot at Appalachia just off Route 2 in Randolph, N.H., might give the appearance of a peaceful rest stop for the travel-weary tourist or late-night trucker. But the initiated know this as a place where high-energy, ambitious hikers retrieve gear from the trunks of their cars as they prepare to start a traverse of the Presidential Range. A full traverse covers just under 23 miles and eight peaks, if you include Mount Clay, which is not an acknowledged 4,000-footer. (To be counted as a 4,000-footer in New Hampshire, a mountain must be separated from a taller neighbor by a col that is at least 200 feet below the mountain's summit. Mount Clay fails this criterion with its higher neighbor, Mount Washington.) Matrosova intends to complete the northern section of the range, which covers 15 miles and five peaks, since she intends to include Clay. Both the long and shorter versions are coveted achievements, especially if accomplished in winter, and there is no shortage of climbing schools and mountain guide services in the region ready to offer support, gear, and tutelage.

Synott Mountain Guides, for example, describes the Presidential Traverse as the "quintessential multi-day mountaineering objective in the East." Other testimonials are similarly effusive: Northeast Mountaineering calls it "New England's single biggest mountaineering challenge"; the International Mountain Climbing School (IMCS) promotes it as "one of the most challenging and difficult mountaineering adventures on the East Coast"; and the Eastern Mountain Sports Climbing School calls it "the classic ridge traverse in the North East." It's clear from these descriptions that to succeed in a winter traverse of the Presidentials, a hiker must be both physically and mentally strong. He or she must also understand and be prepared to deal with the risk involved.

Depending on the size of the group, participants in a Presidential Traverse can pay between $500 and $1,200 for a guided trip. There is also the option of hiring a guide just for you. Depending on which option you choose for the typical three-day, two-night trip, you can sleep up close and personal with the cold and rocky terrain in a mountaineering-specific tent, or elect to sleep at the Randolph Mountain Club's Gray Knob Hut on the first night and at the Mount Washington Observatory on the second. You can also customize your guided trip, crafting an itinerary that works for you. Some hikers, of course, forgo the commercial approach in favor of hiking with companions or, as in Kate Matrosova's case, going it alone.

Hiking alone in the winter Whites can be safe. Brad White of IMCS said as much in an interview with the *Union Leader* newspaper. He added, however, that there are times when bad weather will dictate that you cancel your trip. Winter hikers "need to do some mental math," he said, making calculations about the equipment they have with them and the weather conditions they encounter—or that are forecast. White's IMCS co-owner and accomplished mountaineer Rick Wilcox concurs: "Hiking alone in winter is fine. Even though the general public's perception is that it's suicidal, it's not at all." Wilcox describes Matrosova's itinerary as "an okay plan. She just picked a really, really bad day."

In fact, at 5:00 a.m. that Sunday, the day does not start out badly at all. As Farhoodi and Matrosova approach the Appalachia parking lot, Farhoodi slows the rental car, and makes the left turn into the lot, with dawn still more than an hour away. There are no other cars parked there, an indication that no one has been winter camping at the Madison tent site.

Matrosova retrieves her pack from the back seat and straps into it, then dons the headlamp she'll wear for the next couple of hours as she ascends the Valley Way. Farhoodi plans to head back to their hotel to get some work done while he waits to pick her up at trail's end. As it turns out, the weather at the trailhead is better than what Matrosova has been expecting. The temperature in neighboring Berlin is just below 10°F, and the winds are barely detectable. She is beaming at Farhoodi as she notes the relative mildness of the conditions: It's going to be a good day in the mountains.

It is here that Matrosova begins to be affected by the perception that things will go her way, based on current conditions. She knows full well that it's going to be cold and get consistently colder. But because the early temperature is less cold than she expected it to be, her natural optimism again takes hold. The current winds are minimal, and she still believes that the high gusts will arrive later in the day, allowing time for her to complete her light and fast traverse. As she stands there in the parking lot, the environment appears favorable to her plan.

Matrosova and Farhoodi say their goodbyes, and she walks toward the trailhead, switching on her headlamp. Farhoodi takes his phone out of his pocket and photographs his wife as she makes her

way up and over the high snowbank into the woods and onto the Valley Way. Not long after taking the photo, he will experience a moment many of us have felt when uncertainty floats, unbidden, to the surface. We've all had emotional or physical responses when our instinct or "gut" kicks in and signals trouble or doubt. He waits there for a few moments to see if she might return, that maybe she's changed her mind. But the light of her headlamp never reappears.

Shortly after the tragedy, he will say to journalist Chip Brown, who wrote an excellent account of the incident for *Bloomberg*

BusinessWeek (entitled "Trader in the Wild"), "Every time I said goodbye to her, even if she was just going on her bike with headphones on, I would wonder if I would ever see her again, just because of who she was." But Matrosova had always come back.

So on this day, there is no real reason for Farhoodi to think the trend will not continue. In eleven hours, he'll pull into the Base Road parking lot down off Mount Washington, once again in winter's darkness, and watch for the first signs of the bobbing and swaying beam of his wife's headlamp emerging from the Ammonoosuc Ravine trailhead.

As Matrosova heads up the trail toward Mount Madison, she walks through a very short section of trees and across the Presidential Rail Trail. There she encounters one of the weathered yellow signs that hundreds of thousands of hikers pass by every year in the White Mountains. To those who choose to venture beyond it, the sign's candor offers a glimpse of what might be in store:

ATTENTION

Try this path only if you are in top physical condition,

well clothed and carrying extra clothing and food.

Many have died above timberline from exposure.

Turn back at the first sign of bad weather.

WHITE MOUNTAIN NATIONAL FOREST

We have all encountered such a warning sign, literally in our outdoor venturing or figuratively in daily activities. We are likely to dismiss such a warning, either through inertia or because we overestimate our ability to manage what we are heading into. If you have texted while driving, stood on a chair in your kitchen to retrieve something from a high shelf, or talked politics at a holiday gathering, you've walked by the yellow sign with casual abandon while placing yourself at varying degrees of risk.

Matrosova walks by the sign. As she moves along the snow-covered, well-packed trail, she is likely establishing a flow. Her body temperature is rising as a result of the steady pace she's maintaining, and she's picking out the reflective trail blazes mounted on the trees. Meanwhile, a second message of caution is being posted. But unlike the one Matrosova has just walked past, and unbeknownst to her, this one appears on the website of the Mount Washington Observatory.

Mount Washington Observatory
Summit of Mount Washington
Shortly after 5:00 a.m.

At 5:30 a.m., Ryan Knapp's twelve-hour shift will conclude. Weather conditions at the summit of Mount Washington are mild by Observatory standards. The temperature is -5°F, with a windchill of -34°F, and winds are out of the north at approximately 45 mph. But as the day progresses, the peaceful atmosphere will be invaded by a rowdy, belligerent intruder. Knapp is in the process of typing and posting his Higher Summits forecast discussion for the day, which will read as follows:

> In the clouds with snow and blowing snow, with white-out conditions expected. Temperature starting about 5°F, dropping to about -20°F. Winds from the NE becoming NW at 45 to 60 mph, rapidly increasing midmorning to 80-100 mph with gusts to 125 mph. With severe conditions expected from summits to the valleys, hiking will be extremely risky Sunday through Monday and hiking above tree line is strongly discouraged. If search and rescue needs arise, help will be slow going or postponed until conditions improve. All SAR (search and rescue) assistance if needed will have to come from below, as summit staff will not be able to assist in any way, shape, or form. A single injury will potentially put several lives at risk, not just your own.

In a later interview, Knapp will emphasize the seriousness of his tone in that morning's post: "It's very rare for me to do, but my forecast said don't go above tree line. That weekend's language was the most dire, and the strictest, I've ever written in eleven years of working here." Northeast Mountaineering intern guide Sam Kilburn, who was guiding clients that Sunday on Mount Washington, says, "I remember the post that included mention of the search and rescue teams. It was one of the most extreme but justified warnings I'd ever read." Based on that alert, Kilburn and his group will turn around at tree line that day.

Knapp's Mount Washington Valley forecast discussion warns even those in the lowlands who might be intending to don winter hiking gear:

> [D]riving will be risky today and tonight with white-out conditions expected along roadways and possible downed tree limbs in areas. Wooded areas will also have the risk of falling limbs or trees, so power loss could be experienced. As previously mentioned, blowing snow will also be limiting visibility in all areas of the state too. And as previously mentioned, frostbite and hypothermia risks will be present statewide. So ensure not to have any exposed skin, especially this afternoon through Monday morning.

Virtual alarm bells are sounding throughout Mount Washington Valley, and regions beyond. The Mount Washington Avalanche Center website, which is managed by the National Forest Service (NFS), echoes Knapp's earlier moment of pause for his readers. Snow Ranger Jeff Lane shares the following observation with anyone who might visit the NFS site:

> Mount Washington will truly be putting on a show today and tomorrow. Its well-earned reputation for harsh winter weather will be on display, and I'd recommend taking a seat away from the action for this show. Temperatures will be falling today, reaching -35°F.

> (-37°C) on the summit overnight. During this time, wind speeds will be rising quickly up to the 100-mph (161 kph) mark, with gusts possible reaching 125 mph (201 kph). These conditions are not to be taken lightly. I encourage you to be judicious in your choice of adventure today. Even if your plan

is to stay well below tree line today, bring plenty of warm clothes and extra food and water.

Of course, Matrosova is not aware of either warning, both of which have been posted since she set off. Though she is carrying her cell phone, records show there is no data usage or phone activity during this timeframe. Even if she were to try to use her phone here, there would be no guarantee of a signal.

In addition to her phone, Matrosova is carrying a Garmin 62s handheld Global Positioning System (GPS). This portable unit provides her with information about the terrain and her direction. She has programmed her planned route and has the ability to see trail information on the small screen. But she does not turn on the GPS for the entire length of the Valley Way.

Matrosova likely feels no need for the GPS at this stage because, one month ago, during the Martin Luther King Jr. holiday weekend, she and Farhoodi hiked part of this trail to see how far they could get. That attempt wasn't a spur-of-the-moment thing. They arrived very well prepared, carrying enough gear to camp out in the mountains overnight, in a manner Rick Wilcox might describe as "heavy and slow." They ascended the Valley Way and established camp near Madison Spring Hut. As Chip Brown would report in his *Bloomberg BusinessWeek* article, "The weather was fine by Mount Washington standards: 12°F on the summit, with winds averaging 54 mph."

In his interview with Brown, Farhoodi said he and Matrosova wore insulated, down-filled mountaineering suits and that, between the mild weather conditions and "gear packed for every contingency," he found himself overheating.

That weekend, they spent the night near Madison Hut, and when they arose the next morning, the weather had turned. It was starting to get colder, and clouds were moving in. Matrosova suggested that they aim for one more summit before calling an end to the trip. She wanted to summit Adams. From Madison Col the top of Mount Adams—at only a mile away—is actually quite close. But once you leave the gentle rise of Star Lake Trail and move onto the slope of Adams, you realize the distance is more challenging than it looks, as the steepness starts punishing your legs and taxing your respiratory system.

Farhoodi preferred to descend at that point rather than attempt to reach Adams. The worsening weather conditions and the suffering he had endured the day before on Mount Madison were enough to deter him from going any farther. They were also unfamiliar with the terrain, knowing only what they had gleaned from some research online and in guidebooks. As much as Matrosova wanted to summit Mount Adams, Brown writes, "Whenever she coaxed Charlie into doing something, she was always careful to look after him. They turned back."

Given her drive to succeed at whatever she attempted, this must have been a disappointing moment for Matrosova. The idea of turning her back on what she perceived as an achievable objective—the summit of Mount Adams—must have stung.

Now, one month later, Matrosova is back in her element. She plans to summit Madison, then Adams, and continue south to summit three additional peaks before heading back down to meet Farhoodi at day's end. This time Matrosova is traveling light and fast. She isn't carrying anywhere near the amount or type of gear the couple brought with them last time, and she has no one to answer to but herself. Today's plan will allow her to move at her own pace and make her own decisions, but it has eliminated the benefit of another's voice, another's perspective. She will have only her own judgment to rely on.

Holiday Inn Express
Lincoln, N.H.
6:00 a.m.

Matrosova is one hour deep into the woods on the Valley Way as Erik Thatcher and today's fellow guide, Ben Mirkin, walk into the warm lobby of the Holiday Inn Express hotel to greet their three clients. Just as Thatcher and Alex Teixeira did the day before, he and Mirkin check over their clients' gear to make sure they're wearing the proper clothing and have packed food, fluids, and additional clothing. Taking an inventory before every outing is important, but the task is especially critical today. Thatcher has been watching the weather forecast for days and is laser-focused on it this morning. The gear check concluded, he explains to the group that there is next-to-no chance of summiting Mount Washington today. Thatcher is clear-headed and confident in his decision and offers it with no hesitation, even though he knows his clients may be disappointed. In fact, he receives no push-back at all. Everyone is in agreement that the forecast doesn't bode well for travel above tree line.

With three excited, if somewhat anxious, clients in tow, Thatcher and Mirkin drive about thirty minutes north to the Base Road in Bretton Woods, pulling into the parking lot at 7:00 a.m. They'll hike up the Ammonoosuc Ravine Trail until Thatcher and Mirkin determine they should go no higher. It's the same trail that Kate Matrosova plans to descend in less than twelve hours, when she expects to emerge from the trailhead and meet her husband for the warm ride back to their hotel.

Above Thatcher and his group, at 4,500 feet, the Cog Railway mesonet sensor shows winds just under 15 mph, gusting to 25. The temperature is near 5°F. Just under 1,800 feet above that, on the summit of Mount Washington, the winds are averaging 40 mph and gusting to 60. The temperature at the summit is -10°F.

At 7:16 a.m., as the two guides and three clients make the approximately three-mile hike up "Ammo" to tree line, Thatcher opens the web app on his phone and checks the summit forecast on the Mount Washington Observatory website. He is psyched that his clients are enjoying a small taste of the mountain's infamous weather conditions and captures the moment in a screenshot of the data he sees on the screen:

Sunday:

In the clouds with snow and blowing snow; white-out conditions expected.

Temperature:

High: Starting around 5 below dropping to around 20 below.

Wind: NE shifting NW at 45-60 mph rapidly increasing midmorning to 80-100 with gusts up to 125 mph

Windchill: Falling to 65 below to 75 below

The information is further validation that tree line will not be breached today.

The Bunkhouse
Glen, N.H.
7:00 a.m.

As Thatcher and Mirkin lead their three clients on the early stages of the Ammonoosuc Ravine Trail, Corey Fitzgerald and his intern guide, Sam Kilburn, are conducting a pre-climb briefing with their six clients on the other side of Mount Washington, in the town of Glen. Before the briefing, Fitzgerald opened the web browser on the shop computer, clicked on "Bookmarks" and selected the Mount Washington Observatory website. He already knew what he would see. Like Thatcher, he has been following the weather forecast for days.

Fitzgerald prints a copy of the Weather Observation Report, walks into the common room where his clients are gathered, and reads the report out loud. "There is no chance of a summit today," he says when he is done, making sure to engage each client directly to gauge their reactions. "Getting to Lion Head will be a major achievement. It is way too cold and way too windy," he adds. Like Thatcher, Fitzgerald is always prepared for some degree of push-back from clients, but today he too receives none. "They were remarkably comfortable with the decision," he'll recall later.

The move to alter the plan so early in the day is unusual for Fitzgerald. "On any other day," he says, "I would read the forecast and tell my clients, 'Well, you never know what the weather is until you get up there. We'll go to tree line and stick our nose in it and if we like it, then we'll try for Lion Head and reassess. If we don't like it, we can just turn around.'" Fitzgerald believes it's important to communicate expectations and protocols right at the outset. "If the weather looks bad, I often tell clients ahead of time that we are a team up there, but if I do make a decision to turn around, that decision is final, and I am making it with their well-being in mind. I would be happy to discuss my decision with them once we're off the mountain, but standing in 60 mile-per-hour winds and subzero temperatures is not the place for a debate."

On this Sunday, the decision to turn back has already been made, and there will be no debate. Kilburn and Fitzgerald offer their clients the option of driving over to Appalachia, where Matrosova set off a few hours earlier, suggesting that they go to Madison and "poke our heads above the hut, maybe get [to the summit of] Madison." But all six clients want to start up Washington, even though they know they will not reach the top that day.

The forty-five-minute briefing over, Fitzgerald and Kilburn load their gear into the car and escort their clients fifteen minutes north on Pinkham Notch Road, to the Appalachian Mountain Club's Pinkham Notch Visitor Center. There, the group gathers in the pack room to gear up and make final preparations for the climb.

At 8:30 a.m. they step onto the well-groomed Tuckerman Ravine Trail and head just over two miles south and west toward the Lion Head Trail, along the winter route. The average wind speed at the base of Mount Washington is now just above 15 mph, and the temperature is approximately 7°F. The Lion Head winter route is described in the White Mountain Guide as "the least dangerous route for ascending Mount Washington in winter conditions, and is the most frequently used winter ascent route." After about a half mile of steep inclines, the trail reaches tree line. From there, it is an additional .34 miles to Lion Head.

In later interviews, both Thatcher and Kilburn will say that it is not a bad idea to take clients out in difficult weather conditions, as long as they can be kept safe and as long as they agree in advance that they will turn around when their guides feel it is necessary. "It's the luck of the draw for clients weather-wise," says Kilburn. "You might not reach your end goal, but at least you can show them the beauty of the mountain." Thatcher adds that, even in tough winter conditions, "being below tree line is really safe. If you have clients who have traveled and are already there, you want to do something with them."

The Valley Way
Toward Madison Spring Hut
8:30 a.m.

As the staff at the Mount Washington Observatory monitors the "weather bomb" hovering overhead in its early stages of assembly, Kate Matrosova continues to head upward and is nearing the Valley Way tent site. She has turned off her headlamp and is now making her way in the attenuated winter light. She walks in the shadow cast by Durand Ridge off to her right and is about twenty minutes from reaching tree line. To her left, across the valley from which the trail she's on derives its name, Matrosova might be able to see the upper reaches of the western slope of Mount Madison.

It is not uncommon for hikers on the Valley Way to encounter deep snows as the trees disappear and the lunar landscape of the Presidentials opens up, stark and unsheltered. If you're not wearing snowshoes already, this is where you might need them to push through snow that can reach your waist or even higher. On this Sunday morning, though, Matrosova is enjoying an easier approach to Madison Spring Hut. Her decision to leave her snowshoes at home will not cause a problem yet. It turns out Matrosova has gotten lucky. Rick Wilcox will later explain in an interview with the *Conway Daily Sun* that she "was able to climb up the Valley Way by following a path packed down by snowshoeing climbers two days before."

At 8:50 a.m., as hardwood, tall pine, and conifer give way to their shorter cousin, krummholz, Matrosova breaks tree line and turns on her GPS. In powering up this high-tech compass, she's making a good decision. She's slightly familiar with this landscape, having been here with her husband a month before, and she knows there is an increased risk above tree line of becoming disoriented in the event of a white-out. Later, the GPS will allow investigators to chart her path and offer us a sense of her timing.

South of Matrosova, at 5,300 feet on the slopes of Mount Washington, the temperature is -10°F, and winds at the summit are averaging 45 mph with gusts to 59 mph from the north. As Matrosova makes her way to Madison Spring Hut, she has the wind at her back, which makes the going manageable. At this point, she will encounter a second yellow sign that is meant to serve as the final written warning for hikers heading above tree line:

STOP

THE AREA AHEAD HAS THE WORST WEATHER IN AMERICA. MANY HAVE DIED THERE FROM EXPOSURE EVEN IN THE SUMMER. TURN BACK NOW IF THE WEATHER IS BAD.

WHITE MOUNTAIN NATIONAL FOREST

It is not surprising that Matrosova chooses to continue past this second warning sign. Given the robust winds at her back propelling her forward and the body warmth she has likely built up from her brisk ascent, why would she consider doing otherwise?

At 8:58 a.m., Matrosova arrives at Madison Spring Hut. She is standing at the southwest corner of the boarded-up building and will spend approximately eleven minutes here. During this pause in forward momentum, winter hikers might typically add layers of clothing to maintain body warmth and prevent heat from being drawn away by the winds. They might also have something to eat and drink, for fuel and hydration. But based on the amount of fluids found in her pack the following day, Matrosova is not hydrating enough to replace what she has lost over the past four hours of steadily increased exertion.

V
EXPERIENCE

"Experience is a difficult teacher. She gives the test first and the lesson last."

—*Vernon Sanders Law, former pitcher for the Pittsburgh Pirates*

As Matrosova catches a glimpse of the frozen nitrogen and oxygen concocted by her controlled exhalations during this brief pause in her drive to push through the Northern Traverse, we can take advantage of the moment to reflect on the long, remarkable, and challenging road that has brought her to this place.

She was born in 1982 in Omsk, Siberia, a city in southwest Russia. With a population of just over one million and a long, frigid winter, Omsk is not unlike New Hampshire. In his article for *Bloomberg BusinessWeek*, Chip Brown writes that Matrosova grew up in a poor family, with her parents and a younger sister. Her father served in the Red Army and was decorated for his service at the Chernobyl nuclear power plant disaster of 1986. After completing high school, Matrosova studied finance at Omsk State Transport University.

In 2002, at age 20, she received a work-study visa that allowed her to live and work for a time in the United States. She worked briefly in Montauk, N.Y., before moving to Chicago. Jobs waiting on tables and working as a hostess allowed her to save money so she could hire an attorney to extend her visa. Meanwhile, she pursued her education by taking classes at a community college and was eventually accepted at Chicago's DePaul University. While there, she secured an internship as an equity research intern for Morningstar, a Chicago-based investment firm.

In 2006 Matrosova graduated magna cum laude from DePaul, earning a bachelor of science degree with a major in finance and minors in accounting and marketing. In June of that year, she went to work for J.P. Morgan as a financial analyst and was sent to New York to participate in a six-week training program. There, she met and fell in love with one of her classmates, Charlie Farhoodi, who at the time was a private wealth manager for the company.

In 2008 Matrosova moved to West Palm Beach, Fla., to live with Farhoodi. She continued to work in finance, helping to manage one client's billion-dollar investment portfolio. During her lunch breaks, she would bike to and from the dojo where she trained in Kodokan judo, a 25-mile round trip. Her sensei, Hector Vega, told Chip Brown that he considered Matrosova his "ringer." Vega would instruct his male students, many of whom outweighed Matrosova by 100 pounds or more, to "go defeat that girl, and Kate would thrash them." Once you met her, you would never forget her, Vega said. "Her endurance was incredible. She was really well conditioned."

Vega also told Brown that Matrosova would "never surrender in a match," adding, "She never went halfway on anything. We used to talk about things in life as a judo match, how you have to prepare for possibilities."

According to Brown, Matrosova's "never surrender" ethos would manifest itself when she was placed in a chokehold. This particular hold reduces the amount of oxygen and blood traveling through the neck. The hold is applied to obtain rapid submission from an opponent, which usually occurs quickly, because the affected party feels numbness resulting from decreased blood flow to the face. To signal submission, the losing opponent taps on the mat or the winner's forearm. Either the victor or the referee will stop the match before the opponent loses consciousness. But Matrosova would invariably refuse to tap, according to Vega, preferring unconsciousness to submission.

Throughout this time, Matrosova's tenaciousness and drive to succeed were serving her well, allowing her to thrive in a new country, complete an ambitious degree program, secure lucrative work, and excel at physical challenge. Soon, she would turn her sights to conquering high places.

In 2011, Matrosova climbed her first big peak, the 19,341-foot Mount Kilimanjaro in Tanzania. It was on this climb that her passion for big mountains was ignited. Farhoodi accompanied her on the trip. He later told Brown that his wife convinced him they should forgo porters so they could enjoy the extra challenge of carrying their own gear up the mountain. To prepare for the trip, she taught herself Swahili so she could communicate with the people of the region. Farhoodi said his wife brought with her a suitcase full of toys and games, which she donated to a local school near the mountain.

Matrosova in Tanzania, 2011.

The following year, Matrosova attended the Harvard University Extension School, where she studied numerical analysis and was one of eighty-eight candidates accepted into the highly competitive master's degree cohort at the University of California at Berkeley's Haas School of Business.

While at Berkeley-Haas, Matrosova participated in a project that focused on writing derivative-pricing programs for a Chinese investment bank. One of her teammates on the project was Li Sun, a former Ph.D physicist at Princeton University. Together, Matrosova and Li wrote a program for an options-pricing smartphone app. Li would tell Brown that Matrosova "was an adventurer, but I don't think she was a risk seeker. She wanted to know different things, achieve different things, get to different places. It wasn't about risk. It was about achievement."

It August 2012, Matrosova climbed Mount Elbrus in her homeland of Russia. At 18,510 feet, it is the highest point in Europe.

Matrosova on the summit of Mount Elbrus.

The next year, she and Farhoodi climbed the 14,411-foot Mount Rainier in Washington State, an adventure that also involved participating in a mountaineering course. They learned ice ax and crampon skills, how to dig snow caves to shelter and sleep in, and basic ice and snow anchor work. While high up on Rainier, their group was caught in blizzard-like conditions. With high winds and poor visibility, their guides led them to a wooden shelter to wait out the storm.

The following year, 2014, was a busy one for Matrosova, as she continued to make her mark in the corporate world and in the mountains. She and five of her classmates from Berkeley-Haas competed in the Rotman International Trading Competition in Toronto, Canada. At the conclusion of the competition, the largest of its kind in the world, Matrosova and her team emerged as the highest-ranking team for the United States.

Linda Kreitzman, executive director and assistant dean of the Master of Financial Engineering Program (MFE) at Berkeley-Haas, shared her thoughts about Matrosova's time in the program with Bloomberg.com reporter David Henry: "[Kate] was an inspiration to the Berkeley MFE Class of 2014 and to us all. She was very smart and humble, everyone's friend, and the most down-to-earth and unpretentious individual I have ever had the privilege of knowing and coaching in my fifteen years at Berkeley." Kreitzman shared similar thoughts with Chip Brown in a subsequent interview:

> I'm afraid I'll never find a student like her again. She had a prolific mind, and it wasn't just for finance. It's the immigrant's story. You have to work so hard. She was born determined, and there was no hidden agenda. You see that quality in children. You loved her? Guess what, she loved you back. I know people say, "There she was quantifying risk in her profession. Why didn't she quantify the risk in the mountains?" But she is the only person I know who could try to do what she did. And I know she is not a person who would ever say, "Let me defy death."

In her enthusiasm and drive, the mountains Matrosova was climbing were getting higher, and so, too, were her aspirations. In January 2014, prior to completing her studies at Berkeley-Hass, she climbed Mount Aconcagua in Argentina. At 22,838 feet, it is the highest mountain on the South American continent. While at Aconcagua Base Camp, Matrosova became friendly with another climber, Olya Lapina. In an interview with Chip Brown, Lapina offered her perspective on Matrosova and the mountains:

> It's really important to understand what she stood for and who she was. She wasn't a silly girl playing at mountaineering. She was brave. There are people who push limits and boundaries. Kate had a power within her. Her climbing was leading up to what she would become. It was a way for her to understand and strengthen who she was.

That March, after successfully summiting Aconcagua, Matrosova graduated from Berkeley-Haas with a master's degree in financial engineering. Shortly after graduating, she summited the highest peak in North America, the 20,310-foot Denali (also known as Mount McKinley) in Alaska. For the Denali trip, Farhoodi bought his wife a ResQLink Personal Locator Beacon (PLB) from ACR Electronics. Matrosova didn't take the beacon on the Denali trip because the area she would be in was very remote and she would have the security of being part of a large group. As it happened, the Denali trip lasted much longer than planned because of adverse weather conditions. After a successful summit, Matrosova's group would spend two extra weeks on the glacier waiting for the weather to improve so they could be flown off safely.

Not long after her return from Denali, Matrosova went to work on Wall Street for BNP Paribas, the fourth-largest investment bank in the world, where she had interned a year and a half earlier in its corporate and investment banking unit. During her internship, in December 2013, Matrosova gave an interview with a Berkeley-Haas publication about her experience at BNP. Originally, BNP had planned to place Matrosova on the foreign exchange sales and trading desk, but early on, her mentor saw an opportunity to expose her to different departments within the company. Over the course of the next seventeen months, Matrosova worked in three different functional areas of the company. Expressing pleasure at the diverse experiences she had been afforded, she said, "It worked out perfectly because my goal is to have as much exposure to the company and to different teams; it's a great opportunity to explore different options. I try to find a new person every day and take them to coffee and shadow them for an hour or so to see what they do. It's amazing what you can learn."

Matrosova's appetite for learning was clearly voracious. In an interview with Bloomberg's David Henry, John Karabelas, the head of North American Credit Sales for BNP, said of Matrosova: "Very strong personality, very outgoing, brilliant. It's not surprising, given her personality and her tenacious attitude at work, that she would also do [mountaineering] activities in her free time."

While one might think that the rigors of investment banking coupled with summiting five significant peaks in four years might quench Matrosova's thirst a bit, in her mind, she was just getting started. After reading *Into Thin Air*, the best-selling book by Jon

Krakauer about a dramatic tragedy on Mount Everest in 1996, Matrosova set her sights on climbing Everest. In fact, that goal was one of the factors that brought her to the Northern Presidential Traverse. She saw it as training for an eventual climb to the daunting 29,029-foot peak.

Matrosova also read the book *Minus 148 Degrees*, by Art Davidson, an account of the first winter ascent of Denali, which led her to want to become the first woman to summit Denali in winter.

Earlier, Matrosova had set a goal of climbing the Seven Summits, the highest peaks on each of the seven continents. Having already completed four, she was well on her way to success. In order to achieve her ambitious mountaineering goals, she was constantly working on maintaining her elite level of physical fitness. Leading up to the Northern Presidential Traverse, she was ascending forty-two flights of stairs nearly every day in the Wall Street high-rise where she worked—while carrying a sixty-pound backpack.

It is significant to note that all five of the high-summit climbs Matrosova accomplished from 2011 to 2015 were commercially organized outings led by professional mountain guides. When guided, a client is relieved of the decision-making responsibility. While there is a degree of personal responsibility on the part of each client for self-care, proper use of technical climbing equipment, and general safety practices, professional guides are continuously monitoring and managing their clients, the risks associated with the terrain, and the unpredictability of mountain weather.

"Most of the job is really coaching people on what to expect and when they should do certain things," says mountain guide Corey Fitzgerald. "We're also there in case something goes wrong. That's a big part of climbing. Everyone wants to learn 'hard skills,' but it's the [lapses in] 'soft skills' that kill people in the mountains. When you're guided, you don't necessarily have to think. The guide assumes the soft skills, and does the thinking for you."

Mastering technical (hard) skills involves training, focus, and repetition. But honing soft (decision-making) skills requires a high level of self-awareness and reflection and an ability to manage your emotions. Weak soft skills can lead you to exceed your technical competency.

Guide Adrian Ballinger of Alpenglow Expeditions in Olympic Valley, Calif., discussed the guide/client dynamic in an interview with Ben Schenck of the podcast MtnMeister. "I am very, very conservative in my mountain playing time, especially when I'm working with people who have hired me to minimize that risk," said Ballinger. "We [say] that there is no getting rid of the risk. But it's certainly our job as guides and as a guiding company to minimize or mitigate as much risk as we can and then try to clearly explain those risks that we can't take away."

Ballinger, who has summited 8,000-meter peaks thirteen times, including Mount Everest seven times, has developed a clear-eyed view of risk: "We guides turn around a lot, we go down a lot, we back off a lot, and I really believe that's our job."

It is impossible to know if Matrosova had considered and rejected hiring a guide for her Northern Presidential Traverse. Given the relatively easy experience she had while hiking with her husband the month before, she might not have felt the range demanded a guide, especially when compared with the much higher peaks she had summited in more remote parts of the world. She might have thought she had reached a strong enough stage in her skill level to permit her to go it alone. Or, she might have felt a solo hike would offer her a chance to hone her own decision-making skills.

We know Matrosova was highly self-confident—with reason— and that she had a track record of sound decision making and high performance in her professional career. But if she was relying on her business acumen to make up for her lack of decision-making experience in alpine terrain, she was potentially setting herself up for trouble. At this point in her mountaineering trajectory, Matrosova did possess many of the technical skills necessary to complete her day's objective. She was proficient in the use of crampons and ice ax and in the digging of a snow cave, among other skills. But she had yet to know what it feels like to navigate alone in high winds and white-out conditions, or to independently identify the multiple risks associated with winter terrain.

Self-care truly becomes self-care when there isn't a guide there to remind you of it. Left to her own devices, in an environment known to provide plenty of challenge and risk, was Matrosova capable of controlling her tendency to drive herself to and beyond limits and of lowering her tolerance for suffering? Did she have the soft skills at her disposal to understand when she was exceeding her hard skills? It is not unreasonable to think that, given her past and her personality—both of which were extraordinary—Matrosova was vulnerable to errors in judgment when she set off up the Valley Way that morning.

We can acquire knowledge and experience through self-study, but when the margin for error is thin or the learning curve is steep, regardless of our profession or pursuit, active mentorship becomes a critical factor in success. Mark Richey is a renowned climber who has summited Everest and was a member of the first team to summit the second-highest unclimbed mountain in the world, Saser Kangri II in the Karakorum. In an interview with MtnMeister's Ben Schenck and Russell Wilcox, son of Rick Wilcox, Richey talked about the mentors who played an important role in his early climbing career. With the benefit of this early and ongoing tutelage, Richey has reached a point where he is considered an expert in all aspects of climbing. Over the years, having accomplished much in his climbing and professional careers, he has himself become a mentor to others. "I think part of finding good mentors is making yourself available to people who find an interest in you, and to do that, you have to be someone who is eager to learn," he says. A good mentee, he says, is someone who is not afraid to admit mistakes, someone who is respectful of the people who may be more experienced.

Matrosova was clearly avid to learn in all aspects of her life. But as she approached the White Mountains, she was relying on printed sources rather than on people who could have shared with her their own experiences—including their mistakes—in this unpredictable terrain and offered her a degree of mentorship. The guides on her previous climbs made the decisions for her and their other clients. Mentors, on the other hand, help you develop the "soft skills" for yourself. Had she been hiking under the influence of a trusted White Mountain mentor, would her decisions on this day have been different?

VI
AWARENESS

"Accidents typically leave a distinct trail of seemingly inconsequential mistakes. But then, alpinism is rife with instances—both of ascent and disaster—where small things go wrong, apparently unnoticed by the unlucky protagonists."

—*Michael Wejchert from* The Mad Affair

Madison Spring Hut
Madison Col
Feb. 15, 2015
9:09 a.m.

From her resting place outside Madison Hut, Matrosova is preparing to start her ascent of Mount Madison, named after James Madison, the fourth president of the United States. Since she broke tree line at 8:50 a.m., and during her eleven-minute pause, the weather has not changed. The mesonet sensor at 5,300 feet on the Auto Road records the temperature at -10°F. On the summit of Mount Washington, it is -11°F, with a windchill of -49°F. Winds on the summit are in the low 40s and gusts from the north are 59 mph. For now, the weather system appears stable.

Back on the move, Matrosova leaves the northwest corner of the hut and walks by the small outbuildings to her left and onto the Osgood Trail. After spending the past four hours hiking through enclosed woods, it must feel good to be in a wide-open space on a direct line to her first summit of the day. Entering the barren landscape that exists above tree line, particularly in winter, can be as intoxicating as reaching the summit it envelops. As if craving warmth, frozen lichens cling tightly to the granite rocks and boulders that inhabit the entire Presidential Range. The stark, frigid landscape seems freeze-framed as it waits through the long winter months for the trickling water that will eventually announce spring's renewal. The green of the scrubby krummholz, huddling in random groups, provides the only color, as snow covers the landscape in a thick blanket of white. Trail signs and cairns, redesigned by wind and snow, dot the landscape like rime sculptures. But what you notice above all in winter is the stillness—not only do you leave behind engine noise, electrical currents, and text message alerts, but you don't even hear birdsong or the buzz of insects. You are in a place of absolute remoteness.

While it's easy to lose yourself in the magnificence of such a rare landscape, there is danger in its beauty. For one thing, the little trees that are too short to pierce the thickest snow stand poised to trap the calf or quadriceps of an unsuspecting—or unprepared—hiker. There is always a degree of risk in any environment we find ourselves in, whether at sea level or in high places, but the Northern Presidentials in winter offer a particularly compelling example of the value of situational awareness.

Situational awareness, a skill we should all learn in order to manage risk effectively, allows us to identify potential hazards in our path and either mitigate them or avoid them. To stay safe in unstable and unfamiliar conditions, Matrosova will need to balance the bliss she is likely feeling in these mountains with an equal amount of reasoned calculation. Today, as the weather begins to worsen, she will be called upon to match the spiritual connection she has made to this landscape with a hard-headed approach to the risk it presents.

As defined by the Mountain Rescue Association (MRA), situational awareness is "the degree of accuracy by which one's perception of his/her current environment mirrors reality." Based on a model developed by Dr. Mica Endsley, the association identifies three stages of situational awareness: perception, comprehension, and projection. An engineer by trade and former chief scientist of the U.S. Air Force, Endsley applies a central question to each of the stages she has identified:

Level 1 Awareness: What are the critical factors in the system (Perception)?

Level 2 Awareness: What do those factors mean when integrated with goals (Comprehension)?

Level 3 Awareness: What does it mean over time (Projection)?

In Matrosova's situation, these questions might translate to: 1) What weather am I experiencing and how is it making me feel? 2) Do I need to adjust my plan for the day to avoid getting overtaken by extreme weather that could be coming in faster than I expected it would? 3) Given my gear, my supplies, and my energy exertion to this point, how far can I get before I need to consider turning back or using one of my bailout options?

In another approach to situational awareness, Laura Adams, a certified guide, safety specialist, and avalanche forecaster, identifies three components of a system that influences decision making in avalanche terrain in her three-part series entitled *Avalanche Judgment & Decision Making*. At the moment, Matrosova is not in a section of the White Mountains that carries an avalanche risk, but the factors Adams cites are relevant to her situation—and to our own encounters with risk, wherever we may find them. The influencers, or factors, that make up Adams's system are what she terms the human, the physical, and the environmental.

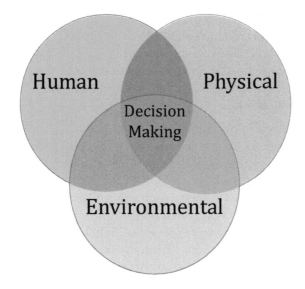

Adaptation of Laura Adams's diagram from *Avalanche Judgment and Decision Making*.

Human factors are the behaviors we bring with us, including our degree of experience, our technical competency, and our emotional reponses. Physical factors include the terrain we are in and the equipment we bring to help us navigate it. Environmental factors include weather conditions and the way they are affecting both us and the terrain.

As shown in the Venn diagram, each critical factor can stand on its own but can also integrate with the others. When we are engaged in decision making, we are considering the point at which all three factors—human, physical, and environmental—integrate. As factors in one part of the system change, other parts of the system will be affected. For example, if high winds cause you to lose electricity at work (a factor of the environmental part the system), your email will stop working (affecting the physical part of the system), which will, in turn, have an impact on your performance (the human part of the system). In the mountains, if you encounter white-out conditions (environmental), as you ascend a steep slope (physical), you can become exhausted and disoriented (human).

As critical factors change and influence one another, what happens to your pursuit of your goals? Do you need to adjust your plan in some way before moving ahead? Have you built the kind of flexibility into your plan that will allow you to adapt to changes in circumstances? Are you under external or self-induced pressure to accomplish your task? Are your emotions influencing your decision? These are the questions you must ask yourself as you move into decision-making mode.

You also need to consider the impact of time on the situation you are encountering. As the critical factors change and affect each other, what do you think things will look like five minutes from now? Thirty minutes from now? One hour from now? Knowing the critical factors and how they're interacting with each other is an incomplete exercise if you haven't projected your situation into the future and forecasted a potential outcome. Making a decision based only on the present moment is a contributing factor in many accidents. To stay safe, you must learn enough about your environment, your terrain, and yourself to imagine what could happen that might influence the situation, your goals, and the overall outcome.

Conrad Anker, in an interview with ultra-endurance athlete Rich Roll, refers to this imaginative leap as "hyper-situational awareness." Anker, a world renowned mountaineer, author, and member of the first team to successfully climb the Shark's Fin on Meru in the Himalaya, describes how he benefits from considering possibility: "I'm thinking about a worst-case scenario and then planning about it in reverse." Anker's approach highlights the importance of Dr. Endsley's third level of situational awareness, "projection," or "What does it mean over time?" Whether he is scaling a mountain or driving his car, Anker is factoring in his next, short-term move and thinking about what could happen in the larger system as he moves through it over the longer term. He is essentially thinking about what the critical factors mean over time, and working his way backward.

This approach is similar to what Gary Klein, a research psychologist who has done extensive study on "naturalistic decision making," refers to as the "pre-mortem." In Klein's model, you undertake a pre-mortem exercise before you set off on a planned course of action. You imagine that the plan has been implemented and has ended in failure or disaster. Then you figure out what factors led to its failure. In formal exercises, those learning Klein's approach work as teams and enjoy the benefit of multiple perspectives. Matrosova is alone. It is impossible to know if, as Anker and Klein would, she is imagining a worst-case scenario and working backward from there. But given the sunny optimism of her personality and her drive to "get there," it seems unlikely that she would adopt a pre-mortem style of thinking.

Situational awareness is a very effective, systematic approach to identifying the potential for complications and risk, and planning how you will manage them. The more complex a system—and the factors at play within it—the more vulnerable it is to complications and negative outcomes.

As Matrosova makes her way up the higher reaches of Madison, she is entering a very complex system in which factors involving weather, terrain, gear, and behavior will all be challenged to the fullest extent, affect each other markedly, and compromise the goals she has set for herself. She is moving in tight, serpentine patterns as she navigates the terrain, trying to stay to the leeward side and avoid the brunt of the 59-mph gusts coming from the north.

At 9:37 a.m., she is 254 feet short of the Madison summit and turns off her GPS, probably to preserve its battery life for later, when she will be navigating unfamiliar areas of the range. It's possible she continues up to the peak after shutting off the GPS. Or, she may stop short to avoid the fully exposed summit and the strong headwinds. If she looks at her Suunto watch, she knows she's an hour and thirty-seven minutes behind the meticulous schedule she drew up for the day, including the thirty minutes she initially lost by starting later than planned. Having already ascended to this summit a month before, maybe she sees this as an opportunity to make up some time. Been there; done that, she may be thinking. We'll never know.

Matrosova is now standing at virtually the same height as the mesonet sensor on the Auto Road. The temperature at 5,300 feet is holding at -10°F, but that will soon change. Winds on the summit of Mount Washington are in the low-to-mid-40s, and gusts have increased by one mile per hour to 60. It is windy and cold, but the environment Matrosova is in has remained largely unchanged since she broke tree line forty-seven minutes ago. The tracks of her ascent are probably still visible, so she is able to follow them back down toward Madison Spring Hut, but she can't see the hut through the fog and dense, blowing snow, with visibility about one-eighth of a mile.

N.H. Fish and Game Department Region 1 offices
Lancaster, N.H.
Sunday, Feb. 15, 2015
10:00 a.m.

As Matrosova descends Mount Madison, some 20 miles away Sgt. Mark Ober, a conservation officer for the New Hampshire Fish and Game Department, sits at his desk entering the details of yet another snowmobile accident into the department's computer database. If he wanted to, he could complete the task with his eyes closed, for this is one of hundreds of accidents involving an off-highway recreational vehicle (OHRV) he and his fellow conservation officers investigate each year. Winter, spring, summer, fall. Any day of the week, any time of day, it is the quintessential "time suck" for this ten-year veteran. Yet Ober loves his job and finds it personally and professionally rewarding. He enjoys working outdoors with a multitude of "tools" at his disposal: a boat, an ATV, a snowmobile, and some really nice mountaineering gear he uses as a member of the search and rescue team. It's the desk work, the administrative stuff, that drives him nuts. And he's not alone. From sworn conservation officer up to colonel, Fish and Game officers prefer to be working out in the field. But as Ober looks out his office window and into the parking lot, he acknowledges to himself that this is one of those days when it's actually nice to be inside. When he signed on duty an hour ago, it was 0°F, and he knows it's going to get a lot colder and gustier. He recalls thinking to himself, "I hope it's quiet today," and resumes typing.

Mount Madison
10:15 a.m.

Matrosova is descending the mountain slowly. Whether she's post-holing (sinking into mini-crevasses of deep snow), or being jostled by wind gusts spiraling over and around Madison, it's taking longer to go down than it did to go up. As she gets closer to the hut, she is approaching a moment when she'll have to make a series of decisions involving the weather (environment), the upcoming terrain (physical), and her ability to perform at the necessary level (human) in this system. There are a number of factors that might influence her decision, and one of them is the possibility of the onset of hypothermia.

Wilderness medicine practitioners and backcountry experts refer to hypothermia as "the silent killer in the backcountry." It is considered "silent" because its victims are unaware that they're slowly falling into a waxy cognitive abyss. The *Wildcare* textbook defines hypothermia as "[t]he lowering of the body's core temperature to a level where normal brain and muscle functions are impaired. It typically happens when several things occur simultaneously: low temperatures (40°F and lower), wet conditions (damp clothes), lack of fuel and hydration (food and water), and physical fatigue. This cascade of problems causes our thermoregulatory system to fail; it just can't keep up with the heat loss."

Though core body temperatures can vary slightly, a temperature of less than 97.7°F is considered abnormal. In the well-below-zero temperatures Matrosova is in, she could potentially lose one degree of her core temperature for every half hour she remains in these conditions.

But as she returns to Madison Spring Hut from the summit of Madison, it is impossible to know how much the cold is affecting her at this point or to gauge whether or not she is already in the early stages of the hypothermia that will later overcome her.

When she arrives back at the hut, she moves to the leeward side of the building and out of the wind, which is rolling straight through

Madison Col. At 10:23 a.m., she turns her GPS device back on. While it took her twenty-eight minutes to ascend Mount Madison from the hut, it has taken her forty-four minutes to descend the same distance. Why did the descent take longer? Post-holing? Wind? In her itinerary, Matrosova has scheduled one hour to hike the 1.4 miles from the summit of Madison to the summit of Adams. It has taken an hour and fourteen minutes to ascend and descend a total of .8 miles on Madison, and Adams is still an hour or more away. She has been at Madison much longer than she planned.

From inside the main compartment of her backpack, she removes the GoPro camera that's taped to the homemade selfie stick Farhoodi made for her. At approximately 10:25 a.m., she takes two photographs of herself. To the casual observer, the digital images reveal no obvious trouble. But a closer look offers reason for concern. The eyelashes of each of her eyes are covered in thick frost. On each cheek there are

prominent, opaque patches of frostbite, and redness that continues onto the bridge of her nose. It appears from these physical signs that she has elected not to wear her goggles since breaking tree line. In windy and cold conditions above tree line, goggles provide vital protection for the eyes and the skin surrounding them. Matrosova is also wearing a neck gaiter pulled up over her mouth to mitigate heat loss. The gaiter is covered in a layer of frost from her exhalations, and if it isn't already frozen solid, it soon will be. She is wearing multiple insulating layers, in fact almost every piece of clothing she's brought with her, but with her face exposed to the extreme elements, she is still losing vital body heat. The frostbite evident on her cheeks indicates that ice crystals have formed in the spaces between the cells below her skin. In the photos, it is impossible to know if she's smiling or experiencing some other emotion.

According to Dr. Murray Hamlet, the retired director of the U.S. Army Cold Research Division and an expert in cold-weather physiology, if Matrosova is able to take photographs, at this stage she still has a way to go before she will truly enter hypothermia. So, what if she isn't experiencing the early stages yet? There may be other influencing factors in play at this point. She stands there alone, the cold winds pouring through the deep glacial cut in the ridge forcing her to steady herself. At the intersection of emotion and reason she is pondering her next move. She has only two choices. If she turns right and heads back down the Valley Way, she can return in the future and try the traverse again. If she turns left onto the Star Lake Trail, she will head into an area that she hasn't been to before.

Nobel Prize-winning psychologist Daniel Kahneman, a provocative theoretician in the area of judgment and decision making and author of the best-selling book *Thinking, Fast and Slow*, would describe Matrosova as having to apply either System 1 or System 2 thinking. According to Kahneman, System 1 "operates automatically and quickly, with little or no effort and no sense of voluntary control." It will produce judgments or decisions based on "suggestions, intuitions, intentions, impressions, and feelings." If Matrosova is having an emotional reaction to the thought of once again abandoning her plan to summit Mount Adams, as she had to do the month before when she was with Farhoodi, she's in System 1.

System 2, on the other hand, engages "the conscious, reasoning self." If your System 2 thinking agrees with what your System 1 thinking has generated, it will turn your impulsive responses into "voluntary actions." While you might believe you spend most of your time in System 2—that you're always rational—Kahneman asserts that System 1 "is more influential than your experience tells you, and it is the secret author of many of the choices and judgments you make." But it is System 2's job to "overcome the impulses of System 1" and apply "self-control."

The main challenge for System 2 thinking, however, is that your capacity to mobilize it can be depleted if you are in a state of physical exertion, extreme stress, or exhaustion. According to Kahneman, time pressure is another important factor. If Matrosova is pushing herself to make up time and is worried about the impact further delay will have on her goal of getting off the mountains before dark, she's taxing her ability to engage in System 2 thinking. She might be aware of deteriorating weather conditions but more compelled by her strong desire to succeed. "Several psychological studies have shown that people who are simultaneously challenged by a demanding cognitive task and by a temptation are more likely to yield to temptation," writes Kahneman. "Activities that impose high demands on System 2 require self-control, and the exertion of self-control is depleting and unpleasant." If System 2 thinking is too exhausting for you, guess which system wins out?

Joe Arvai, the director of the Erb Institute at the University of Michigan and a Max McGraw Professor of Sustainable Enterprise, is also a climber and has done extensive research on the psychology of decision making and risk. In an interview for the "Out There" podcast, Arvai states that when we are under stress, or excited, System 1 takes on additional weight and needs more data to attain balance. Arvai explains that, during these moments, your emotional self needs "solid data" in order to make a rational decision. But Arvai expresses caution as well: "In the mountains, even though you might be presented with data, that visceral pull is just so powerful, you can't beat it back."

In his book *Surviving The Extremes: A Doctor's Journey to the Limits of Human Endurance*, Dr. Kenneth Kamler, a mountaineer and the only physician on Mount Everest during the 1996 disaster, offers further commentary on the brain science behind decision making: "It is no surprise that emotions can easily override logic. [...] Emotions can prevail over reasoning because the pathways from the amygdala emotion center to the cingulate decision center are very well developed. They carry more signal traffic, and thus more influence, than the less developed pathways (of the brain) that go in the other direction. Emotional impulses can overwhelm the capacity for reasoning far more easily than logical control can be exerted over primitive responses."

So System 1 thinking often wins out, emerging from what Kahneman calls our "biases." One of these biases is "regret avoidance," which often leads us to make a wrong decision because we anticipate feeling regret if choose another option. Might Matrosova have felt regret the month before when she didn't climb Adams? Is she worrying that she will feel even more regret if she fails to do it this time, too?

"Confirmation bias," according to Kahneman, is our tendency to interpret incoming information as confirming our existing beliefs. In his book *Normal Accidents*, Charles Perrow writes that "we construct an expected world because we can't handle the complexity of the present one, and then process the information that fits the expected world and find reasons to exclude the information that might contradict it." Arvai expands on that concept when he says, "[P]eople tell themselves stories to justify their position. [...] We convince ourselves of certain things and then search for evidence to validate our position." The winds are strong where Matrosova is standing, but might she believe they are not as strong as she expected them to be? Mount Adams is only a mile away and much lower than peaks she has reached before. How hard can it be to get there?

We are also vulnerable, according to Kahneman, to making decisions based on the "sunk cost effect." This is what he calls our tendency to escalate our commitment to our current course of action because we've invested time and/or money in it and feel that anything less than reaching our original goal will constitute failure. This pitfall was evident during the well-publicized and documented 1996 Everest disaster, as guides and clients continued toward the summit long after the agreed-upon turnaround time. In an interview with Kathryn Schulz of *Slate*, Ed Viesturs, who has climbed all fourteen of the world's 8,000-meter peaks without supplemental oxygen, talked about the effect of the "sunk cost effect" on climbers he has known: "I've seen it many times," he said. "And I'd always thought, it doesn't matter how long you've been there, how much money you've spent, how much energy you've expended. If the situation isn't good, go down. The mountain's always going to be there. You can always go back." Is Matrosova thinking to herself that she and Farhoodi have made the long drive from New York for the second time in thirty days, and she needs to make that commitment worth it?

We can also succumb to what Kahneman calls "overconfidence bias," our tendency to think we know more about something than we actually do. In his *Slate* interview, Viesturs discusses why it can be risky to think that past experience will guarantee future success, especially if you have built that experience under the expert guidance of a seasoned professional who is making all your decisions for you: "You can't make a mistake if you aren't the one making the decision," he said. "When I meet a group of clients before a climb, I say, 'Here's the deal: It doesn't matter how much money you've paid to climb this mountain. I will make all the decisions. I'll let you know when I'm making them and why I'm making them, but in the end, you are hiring me to make the decisions, because I have the experience to do so.'" Is Matrosova relying too much on her guided climbs of higher summits, the mountaineering course she took on Mount Rainier, and her impressive track record of high performance at work? Do all those transfer to the situation she finds herself in today?

Finally, Kahneman identifies something he calls "recency bias." This is our tendency to give too much weight to recent outcomes when making a decision. Laurence Gonzales, author of *Deep Survival: Who Lives, Who Dies, and Why,* refers to these outcomes as "bookmarks," and writes, "The brain creates such bookmarks (technically known as 'somatic markers,' a term coined by Antonio Damasio) because logic and reason are much too slow if we are going to get around in this big old goofy world." Gonzales explains that we use bookmarks in cases where decisions must be made quickly: "The emotional system [Kahneman's System 1] reacts to circumstances, finds bookmarks that flag similar experiences in your past and your response to them, and allows you to recall the feelings, good or bad, of the outcomes of your actions. Those gut feelings give you an instant reading on how to behave. If the previous experience was bad, you avoid that option. If it was good, 'it becomes a beacon of incentive,' to use Damasio's words." Standing in temperatures well below zero, and way behind schedule, Matrosova must be feeling a sense of urgency. She has encountered wind and cold in the mountains before, but on her biggest climbs, she has always been able to reach her summit goal and has experienced the good feelings those successes engendered. "Those feelings," writes Gonzales, "will more or less force a decision unless checked by a higher consciousness" [Kahneman's System 2]. If Matrosova is locked into System 1 thinking, she might very well be reflecting on the summits she's reached in the past four years and wondering why the outcome of this trip should be any different.

Turn right and go back down the mountain? Push ahead and try for Adams? This might seem to us like an obvious decision, knowing what we do about the forecasts and warnings, but in Matrosova's circumstances, it must have seemed very complicated. Matrosova does

have access to data that would add weight to System 2. It's colder and windier than when she first broke tree line almost two hours ago, so she knows it's getting tougher, but she also likes to embrace challenge. She is known as a rational thinker and is well aware that the trip has taken her longer than expected. It has taken her five and a half hours to cover 4.4 miles. There are still 10.6 miles remaining in her planned itinerary. If her rate of ascent and descent remains consistent—that is, if the weather, the terrain, and her strength remain favorable—it will take her another thirteen hours to reach Base Road at Ammonoosuc

Ravine. By sunset at 5:17 p.m., she will likely be somewhere between Mount Clay and Mount Washington, still above tree line and soon to be hiking in complete darkness, a possibility she has tried to avoid with her light-and-fast plan.

Based on the data she has at her disposal, she has probably written off the remainder of the traverse at this point. Perhaps she feels that decision will allow her to avoid the greatest risk she is facing. Perhaps that assumption allows her to believe there is minimal risk in continuing for one more hour over to Mount Adams before turning back. She may see a cost in aborting her original plan but a benefit in being able to summit Adams. Matrosova is extremely well equipped—mentally, physically, and intellectually—to handle challenges and risk, but here she may be underestimating how quickly and devastatingly the White Mountains can smother those hard-earned attributes.

In her original plan, Matrosova thought she would call Farhoodi from her satellite phone after descending Mount Madison to check in with her time and location, and to get any pertinent updates on weather. But they both decided she should forgo that call to preserve the battery life of her phone in the event she got into trouble farther along the range.

As she stands at her decision point, Matrosova needs a rescuer. Not the kind who will be searching for her in mere hours, but a hand-on-the-shoulder kind of savior, someone to say, "Not today." Right now, she needs a System 2 thinker. While her need to project her thinking forward and see potential disaster ahead might seem obvious to us, it isn't to her. In his book *The Undoing Project*, Michael Lewis quotes Daniel Kahneman and his longtime collaborator, the late Amos Tversky, on the importance of honing our imaginative powers when we are faced with a critical decision: "We often decide that an outcome is extremely unlikely or impossible because we are unable to imagine any chain of events that could cause it to occur. The defect, often, is our imagination."

But for our imagination to be effective, it must be able to draw on similar experience. In his book *Desperate Steps: Life, Death, and Choices Made in the Mountains of the Northeast*, author Peter Kick echoes Kahneman and Tversky, and brings the issue closer to Madison Col: "Being prepared means, in essence, using your imagination to determine what is conceivably possible, even though it may seem unlikely. What can possibly happen in an area you're headed for? What can possibly happen based on your level of physical fitness? What might happen based on chance, and still lay within the realm of possibility?" Matrosova's experience in the White Mountains has been so minimal—one weekend in benign winter weather—that she may not be able to imagine just how rugged and demanding this terrain can be, particularly when she is alone.

Winds on Mount Washington are now averaging 50 mph and gusting to 70, and the temperature is -13°F with a windchill of -54°F. On the Auto Road, at the 5,300-foot mark, the mesonet sensor shows the temperature at -12°F. The system is changing. Regardless of which way Matrosova goes, she'll need to get moving soon to reload the body heat she's losing rapidly through convection.

At 10:27 a.m., with the winds acquiring greater traction in the atmosphere and the temperature dropping steadily, Matrosova turns away from the safety of the Valley Way and heads toward Mount Adams.

VII
MOMENTUM

"Facts are stubborn things; and whatever may be our wishes, our inclinations, or the dictates of our passions, they cannot alter the state of facts and evidence."

—*President John Adams*

Madison Col
Feb. 15, 2015
10:27 a.m.

Star Lake is a shallow tarn about .2 miles south of Madison Spring Hut. It was named in 1875 by Moses Sweetser, editor of the Randolph Paths guidebook, because, in his words, "it mirrors so perfectly the constellations above." Not today, however. Today it is frozen solid. Had it not been frozen, Matrosova might have seen her reflection in it, thick frost caking her eyelashes, frostbite on her cheeks.

It's now 10:33 a.m., and she has made good time since leaving the hut a few minutes before. At the edge of the tarn, she continues to her right, around the western side of the frozen water. She is gaining momentum through here as she moves closer to the steeper slopes of Mount Adams. Winds on the summit of Mount Washington are now averaging 53 mph, and gusts are between 70 and 80. The winds remain at her back through this area, but gusts will still blow toward and around her.

It is typical to associate momentum with positive action. The quarterback completes a long pass, the players continue down the field seemingly effortlessly, and everyone expects they'll score a touchdown. But momentum can sometimes turn counterproductive, and that may be what is happening to Matrosova at this point.

Michelle Barton and Kathleen Sutcliffe, in their essay "Learning When to Stop Momentum," published in the MIT's *Sloan Management Review*, identify five factors that can cause dysfunctional momentum. They draw their findings from wildland firefighting. In one instance that occurred in May 2000, a controlled burn in New Mexico turned into one of the most destructive wildfires in our nation's history, causing $1 billion in damages, scorching 47,000 acres of land, and destroying 300 homes and buildings. Firefighters would think they had extinguished a flare-up, only to have to return again to put out the same fire. Barton and Sutcliffe assert that dysfunctional momentum occurs "when people continue to work toward an original goal without pausing to recalibrate or reexamine their processes, even in the face of cues that suggest they should change course."

Here is a simplified version of the five factors Barton and Sutcliffe identify as contributing to dysfunctional momentum:

Action orientation: We're moving toward a goal, and we either choose to ignore, or miss altogether, complications or problems. This is especially true when we're under pressure or facing a deadline.

Inflexible planning: We've adopted a plan or launched an initiative and we're moving forward. When we encounter a complication or problem, we stick to the plan regardless of the need to adapt.

The ripple effect: Small changes in one part of our plan are likely to affect other parts of the plan as well, but we remain unaware of this development or unresponsive to it.

Rationalization: We respond positively to data that reinforces our belief in what we are doing and ignore evidence to the contrary. We tell ourselves a story that validates our wish to continue on, and wave away red flags.

Deference to perceived expertise (expert halo): We tend to defer to those with authority or those we perceive to have a higher level of expertise than our own.

Though Matrosova is alone and so not prone to the fifth factor, she is vulnerable to the first four. A naturally driven and goal-oriented person, she may remain narrowly focused on her goal to reach Adams this time, despite the strong winds and deteriorating conditions. In fact, she may be reading the conditions more positively because that reading fits better into her plan.

Barton and Sutcliffe recommend two strategies for avoiding dysfunctional momentum: "situated humility" and "interruptions." They write that "[s]ituated humility arises not out of personal insecurity but rather from the acceptance that, however confident one is in his own skills and abilities, the situation is so dynamic, complex, and uncertain that no individual can be fully knowledgeable under the circumstances." In an interview, Barton expanded on this point, saying that people must recognize going into a situation that "it is dynamic and that it will change in ways that are unpredictable." With her track record of success in business and in the mountains, has Matrosova entered this situation in the belief that she can handle anything, however challenging, and if so, has she seriously underestimated just how dynamic these mountains can be in winter?

Barton and Sutcliffe also recommend creating pauses as you work through a plan or process, even when you feel things are going smoothly. "By creating interruptions we can often prevent or overcome dysfunctional momentum in our own situations," they write, an approach that "forces us to reconsider whether we really know what is going on and how well the present actions are working." It's good, they say, to stop from time to time and ask ourselves, "What's the story now?"

At 10:36 a.m., three minutes after leaving the frozen shoreline of Star Lake, Matrosova does, in fact, interrupt her forward momentum. As she leaves Star Lake, rather than staying right and moving onto the slope of Mount Adams toward the summit, she walks straight and a bit down to her left. It's possible she has lost the trail. The winter has seen a lot of snow, which can build up in this area and cover the cairns, sometimes hiding the trail itself. But her pause might be deliberate. Guide Brett Fitzgerald says, "It's a logical place to stop. It's pretty sheltered from the wind without dropping down too far."

Matrosova does stop, for eight minutes. Is she adding layers? Has she decided to put her goggles on? Is she taking a drink of hot tea and having something to eat? Is she disoriented and taking time to find the trail on her GPS? Whatever the reason, eight minutes is a long time to stand still in subzero temperatures amid the high winds that are spilling over Mount Adams above her and through Madison Col.

At 10:45 a.m., she is back on the move. As she picks up the trail again, she briefly walks into a headwind that continues to increase in force. Winds on Mount Washington are averaging 60 mph at this point, and the temperature on the Auto Road at 5,300 feet is -12°F. If Matrosova continues walking straight, responding to the high winds, she'll be back at Madison Spring Hut within ten minutes. A left turn will take her upward and onto the lower slopes of Mount Adams's summit cone. If she has used her pause to reconsider or reevaulate her day's goal, the short hiatus does not deter her from trying to summit Adams. She takes a left turn and heads to the top.

At 11:21 a.m., Matrosova veers off to her right and leaves the Star Lake Trail. If she were to stay on that trail, she would find it actually continues left of the summit cone and wraps around the upper slope of Adams before making a southeastern approach to the summit. But for some reason, Matrosova is electing to take a much steeper and exposed line to the top. Is she trying to get onto the Air Line, where she can follow the ridgeline to the summit? If she reaches the Air Line, will she bail out, turn right, and descend the trail back to Madison Spring Hut? Or is she just trying to gain time and take what might appear to her to be the fastest route to the summit?

Whatever her reasons, she is entering an area with large snowfields and slopes of forty to fifty degrees. This is steep, rocky terrain, and she is making very slow progress. Depending on snow conditions, a hiker here must be wary of post-holing into the deep gaps between boulders that lie hidden under the snow, or of falling and sliding. Brett Fitzgerald describes the area as "really steep, a huge snowfield that's kind of scary. It's really a 'no-fall' zone. It's pretty wind scoured. If you slip, you're sliding a long way unless you self-arrest with an ax." This is terrain that often warrants the use of snowshoes with traction spikes, or micro-spikes, or crampons. Matrosova does not have snowshoes or micro-spikes, and she doesn't choose to use her crampons.

Since rounding the slight bend after Star Lake, she is hiking in the shadow of a geologic wind barrier. Ascending the leeward slopes, she is getting some relief from the winds as they graze the ridgelines above her. Mount John Quincy Adams helps to buffer the gusts. But to imagine that Matrosova is untouched by strong winds is unrealistic. Observatory meteorologist Ryan Knapp will say later in an interview that winds from the north/northwest are traveling up and over and wrapping around the land masses that make up the Northern Presidentials. "Picture a rock in the middle of a brook," he says. "Watch as the water pours over the top of the rock and wraps around it. Now imagine that's how the winds are behaving at Madison Col and Mount Adams."

Knapp adds that such strong, sustained winds sap the energy of a hiker. "When you get hit by strong gusts, it's like being connected to a rope and pulled by a car. The car is going twenty miles per hour, then accelerates to fifty miles per hour, and then decelerates again." This constant push, pull, tug, shove, however you want to describe it, is exhausting."

In an interview with the *Union Leader* following the accident, Brad White, president of the International Mountain Climbing School of North Conway, N.H., echoes Knapp's assessment. "A persistent wind will rob hikers of sense and strength, and higher gusts, those above eighty miles per hour, will stop their forward progress entirely," he says.

Between Mount John Quincy Adams and the higher Mount John Adams, there lies a small col. Knapp explains that, at 11:48 a.m., the northwest winds around Matrosova are "whipping up and over the col, and bringing with them dense blowing snow from the windward slopes." Winds on Mount Washington's summit are gusting to 86 mph, the temperature is -15°F, and the windchill is -59°F. The temperature at 5,300 feet on the Auto Road, at -14°F, is flirting with the reading almost 1,000 feet higher up.

Watching from the Observatory, Knapp describes the wind and blowing snow as a "ground blizzard." This phenomenon occurs when the wind is blowing so hard that it is whipping up the snow as if it's snowing, except it isn't snowing, and visibility is either low or nonexistent. Matrosova is certainly hiking in "full conditions" as she continues up Adams. The higher and more steeply she climbs, the slower she is moving, and the colder she is getting.

Ammonoosuc Ravine Trail
Mount Washington
Noon

Erik Thatcher, Ben Mirkin, and their three clients approach a small forest protection sign that lies one-quarter mile from Lakes of the Clouds Hut, and which announces the end of wooded hiking. They're at tree line, the predetermined turnaround point they identified before leaving the hotel earlier that day. The group has moved slowly up to this point, since there's a lot of snow on Ammo. Thatcher and his team are being toyed with by the strong winds. "You could feel it," Thatcher will recall later. "You could hear the wind above you like a freight train, and as you got closer to tree line, you could feel it more and more." Providing further validation of Knapp's observations, Thatcher adds, "Visibility was low. There was a lot of blowing snow where we were."

Erik Thatcher takes a photo of himself, clients, and fellow guide Ben Mirkin on "Ammo."

Below them, at 4,500 feet, the Cog Railway mesonet sensor is showing the protection afforded by the trees lower down. There, winds are averaging 13 mph and gusting to 25 mph. But Thatcher and team are in the thick of it. At the cusp of tree line, their human sensors are receiving more extreme data. While not experiencing the more than 80-mph gusts at the summit cone above them, they're already feeling much stronger, brisker winds and colder temperatures than are being recorded below them by the Cog sensor.

Will Thatcher and Mirkin succumb to any biases, as emotion (System 1) and reason (System 2) work to achieve some balance? The hut's not far; maybe we'll just take the clients there? After all, our clients paid good money and have driven all the way here. Is tree line a worthy enough achievement? Will they be disappointed with us?

No. Today, System 2 prevails for all involved. Thatcher and Mirkin offer no enticement, and there's no resistance from their three clients. Everyone standing there has all the data they need. Taking one last look at Mother Nature's fury, they turn their backs on the weather bomb, and descend.

Androscoggin Valley Regional Hospital
Berlin, N.H.
Noon

As Thatcher, Mirkin, and their clients descend Ammo, Sgt. Mark Ober stands in the emergency room at Androscoggin Valley Regional Hospital. He's here to interview the victims of yet another snowmobile accident. Of the two options this frigid afternoon, being inside for the interview or riding his snowmobile to investigate the scene of the crash, this may be the winning ticket. Ober asks Conservation Officer Matt Holmes to park his cruiser at Randolph Fire Station and, via the Presidential Rail Trail, respond to the crash scene on his snow machine. Ober takes a statement from the crash victims, collects his paperwork, and drives to Northern Extremes Snowmobile Rentals off Route 302 in Bartlett to collect information on the snowmobile that was damaged in the crash and to obtain a copy of the rental agreement. Time suck, in progress.

Mount Adams
Eastern slope snowfields
12:47 p.m.

Matrosova has reached an elevation of 5,650 feet on Adams, where she is 144 vertical feet from the summit. She can climb no higher, because she's walked headfirst into an impenetrable wall of wind. To paint a picture of the struggle, the Randolph Paths guidebook estimates that it will take a reasonably fit hiker, in normal three-season conditions, one hour to hike the mile from Madison Spring Hut to the summit of Adams, gaining 1,000 feet of elevation. Matrosova left Madison Spring Hut two hours and twenty-one minutes earlier, and has ascended 855 vertical feet.

Since resuming her hike at 10:45 a.m., following her pause off trail, it has taken Matrosova two hours and three minutes to ascend 750 vertical feet, the last 159 of which have taken forty minutes. It's clear that the steep slope, rugged terrain, and brutal winds are having a negative effect on her ability to function as she would like—and as she is used to doing.

A Mount Washington Observatory staff member trying to walk into 70-80 mph winds on the summit of Mount Washington.

If the system Matrosova is operating in were perfect, just thirteen minutes from now she would be arriving at her fourth summit of the day, Mount Clay. But the system is so far from perfect that the chaos makes it impossible for her to visualize what calm might look like. Now, crouching and bracing herself against the 80-plus-mph headwinds pouring over the ridgeline like a dam break, not only is she unable to climb the 144 feet to her second summit, she can make no forward progress at all. Her first bailout point, Gray Knob Cabin, a walk of about fifty minutes from the summit of Mount Adams, is unreachable. From where she is, with a ground blizzard in full force, she is also unable to see the buildings atop Mount Washington, which for her might be a reassuring sign of civilization. This is the hiker's version of being alone and stranded on Mars.

At this point, Matrosova's only option—if she hopes to survive—is to turn and go back, to retreat to what she now must perceive as safety. It is a new goal, and one that will generate a sense of true achievement if she's able to accomplish it. If she can make it back to Madison Spring Hut, she'll be able to descend to the protection waiting for her below tree line.

Slowly, Matrosova turns 180 degrees and puts her back to the 80-mph winds that have been applying so much pressure to her chest that it's been almost impossible for her take full breaths as she has ascended. But even after turning around, she gets little relief from the assault.

Matrosova's decision to turn back is a pivotal moment in her mountaineering trajectory. She has always accomplished everything she set out to do, and retreat must feel unfamiliar to her. It is the right decision, but unfortunately it has come too late. She is now caught in a complex trap set by the colliding forces of Mother Nature, millions of years of glacial retreat, and her own decision making.

As she descends, she must continue to make decisions and manage risk. Is there a contingency plan available to her beyond the bailout options she originally set up? An emergency bivouac could allow her to wait out the storm, but she hasn't brought a shelter with her, she has exhausted her cache of insulated clothing, and a snow cave would be impossible to dig out in this terrain and weather. She must continue to move downward and then toward Madison Spring Hut. She must stay low to the ground, and kneel or lie prone between overwhelming gusts of wind. She must wait for a lull, and then walk or crawl quickly, but carefully, over the difficult terrain. She must continue to move to generate body heat, because stopping for too long will prove fatal in these temperatures.

At this point, Matrosova is not calling it a day and confidently heading back down the mountain. She is, in fact, self-rescuing. Her options are as thin as the margin for error in her original itinerary, which has been destroyed by the weather bomb that she thought would hit much later. As Lt. Wayne Saunders of New Hampshire Fish and Game will later remark in an interview with Nestor Ramos of the *Boston Globe*, at this stage Matrosova "is systematically trying to save her own life."

HOW COLD WILL CLAIM HER

Here are the details of what is likely to occur as Kate Matrosova battles with hypothermia, a struggle she will ultimately lose:

The effects will start when her core temperature drops to below 97.7°F. At that point, her metabolic rate will increase. She will burn more glucose to generate body heat. This will require her to take on more fuel to keep her glucose stores at a level at which her body can continue to generate heat. Her brain, sensing trouble, will take on a defensive posture and reduce the amount of blood flow it sends to her skin, a process known as vasoconstriction. Matrosova's skin, acting as an additional layer of insulation to prevent heat loss, will not receive the blood it needs to preserve that layer of protection. Evidence of this will take the form of frostbite, patches of white on the skin where blood flow has ceased or slowed.

Gradually, Matrosova's judgment will begin to show signs of impairment. This may begin early, as she approaches the intersection of the Valley Way and Star Lake trails and must decide if she will head down or on toward Mount Adams. If she is already in the incipient stage of hypothermia at this point, she'll put greater emphasis on goals she hopes to achieve—the summits she's planning to reach—and less attention on the weather and what's going on around her. Her ability to understand the critical factors of the system she is in will become compromised. The strong spiritual connection Matrosova has always felt in the mountains will also dull as she becomes apathetic to her surroundings.

As guide Corey Fitzgerald has said, self-care is the first thing to go, and Matrosova will struggle with layering her clothing properly and maintaining thermoregulation. She will become inconsistent in her consumption of food and water, and her glucose stores will dip. According to Dr. Murray Hamlet, "You don't have to have too far a drop in core temperature to start making mistakes."

When Matrosova's core temperature drops another degree (to around 96°F) she will enter the stage of mild hypothermia. At this point, her body is doing everything it can to maintain warmth. She will start to shiver, the body's attempt to warm itself through involuntary exercise. Shivering will burn even more fuel and start to fatigue the muscles being used in the process. As she continues to shake, her fine motor skills will be impaired. She will have difficulty holding objects, zipping up her jacket, or taking an item out of her backpack. If she tries to speak, it will sound slow and slurred. She will become very tired. "People become physically and mentally exhausted as they try to get warmer," Hamlet explains. "You have to experience real winds and real cold before you can fully realize the effect it can have on you."

When she reaches even this mild stage, she might consider what we would think of as "common sense" decisions to be an intricate cobweb of options. Hamlet warns those of us who might like to engage in armchair quarterbacking: "You are not in the same setting as the affected person. You're not cold and exhausted when you ask the same question or consider the same decision."

Matrosova's goal-driven focus on reaching the summits and completing the Northern Traverse could smother any thoughts of self-preservation. In Dr. Murray Hamlet's words, "With hypothermia, there's always a mismatch in value between what's driving them up the mountain and driving them down." So as the weather deteriorates and Matrosova is possibly feeling the early effects of hypothermia, she might prioritize her decision to be there—and to continue on—and ignore the need to add additional layers of clothing, even if she feels cold.

Over time, as her core temperature drops further (to around 94°F), Matrosova's shivering will reach its peak. Her metabolism will be in overdrive, and her body will begin burning fuel at a rate that will exhaust any remaining stores within the next four to five hours. She doesn't even realize she's cold. She believes she is thinking rationally, when in fact, she's doing the opposite. She is unable to solve what are normally simple and obvious problems. If she finds herself sliding down a steep incline or battling a spruce trap, she'll be aware of it but unconcerned.

Then, when she finds herself trudging through deep snow, she will be generating ten times more body heat than when at rest. This will produce sweat, which will allow the cold to penetrate more deeply. She will begin to stumble and fall down. If she drifts off trail, she will likely become disoriented and lost. If she slows and stops, she will become even colder, as her perspiration evaporates and is carried away from her body by the winds. If she drops her mountaineering ax or a glove, she won't care. If the summit is above her, she will continue toward it.

At a body temperature of 92°F, Matrosova will be shivering violently. Nothing around her will seem real. She will no longer be walking upright, but instead will crawl toward her intended goal.

At 90°F, she will begin convulsing. The violent spasms will come at one-minute intervals, then stop. The end of her shivering will coincide with the near depletion of her body's glucose. If she tries to speak, she will produce only indecipherable mumbling. As her body tries in vain to hold onto the heat that remains in her core, she will curl into a ball and wrap her arms around herself to decrease her surface area and attempt to preserve warmth. It won't be long before her last stores of glucose are gone, and her shivering stops completely. She is losing consciousness, and may come to the realization that she won't survive this ordeal. But she won't experience fear or panic; she will feel peaceful in her resignation.

With nothing left to protect her, as she lies there defenseless to the cold and wind, with her body temperature down to about 86°F, Matrosova will enter a metabolic icebox. Her system will operate at a minimal level to maintain any vestiges of glucose and preserve oxygen. Her blood will be 190-percent thicker than when she started her hike that morning. Her breathing will slow to three to six respirations per minute, and if rescuers or passersby were to find her at this stage, they might be unable to detect a pulse or breathing. She is comatose and in no pain. She will not respond to either verbal or physical stimulus. Her heart will enter arrhythmia, she will go into cardiac arrest, and she will die.

VIII
COMPLICATIONS

"I find it fascinating that our modern planet has areas where no modern technology can save you, where you are reduced to your most basic—and essential—self."

—*Jean-Christophe Lafaille, mountaineer*

Approach to Lion Head
Mount Washington
1:00 p.m.

As Matrosova is in the early stages of executing her attempt at self-rescue off of Mount Adams, over on Mount Washington, Corey Fitzgerald, Sam Kilburn, and their six clients arrive at tree line. Lion Head, at 5,033 feet, is still up ahead and just what it sounds like—a massive rock formation that stands watch over Tuckerman Ravine, much like a lion does over its pride. Winds through here are some of the strongest on the mountain. It is a wide-open expanse, with nothing to slow the force of the wind as it slams into and wraps around the summit cone of Mount Washington.

The group has stayed together up to tree line. Like Thatcher and Mirkin's group over on Ammo, this group has experienced slow going. "Trail conditions on the route were pretty normal, well packed down," Fitzgerald will say later. "But everything was a little slower that day. There's a pretty steep section on the Lion Head route, but there was nothing out of the ordinary that happened on the hike up."

But Kilburn will recall using heightened thermoregulation practices that day. "I remember starting with a larger number of layers than I normally do," he said. "The winds were really whipping." He added that, as the group made its way on Tuckerman Ravine Trail, the winds, which "are usually calm, were still blowing in the trees." Kilburn recalls that his jacket was covered in frost as perspiration moving through the layers of his clothing froze on the outer shell.

As the group arrives at the point where the winter route rejoins the summer route, Fitzgerald and Kilburn assess the situation. Four of their clients are ready to descend. "For them it's mostly fatigue," says Fitzgerald. "It isn't the wind or anything that's causing them to turn around. They'll turn themselves around without any hesitation."

Kilburn adds, "People have a pretty gung-ho attitude coming in, but once they get in the weather, they start to understand why we have to turn around." This is what Conrad Anker refers to as "patience" or "playing the long game," making a decision to live and climb another day.

While four of the clients decide to descend, the two Fitzgerald instructed at Wiley's Slide the previous day want to continue on to Lion Head, just over three-tenths of a mile and a forty-five minute hike beyond tree line. Fitzgerald and Kilburn agree that Kilburn will take the four clients down, while Fitzgerald continues on with his two. Fitzgerald has had some time to observe his clients and, based on his observations, he is confident that their risk tolerance is in alignment with their level of technical competency, the terrain, and the conditions that lie just above them.

Hikers descending Lion Head (upper left) in favorable conditions.

Risk tolerance can be defined as the amount of uncertainty an organization, team, or individual is prepared to accept in pursuit of goals and objectives. While Fitzgerald has identified the risks associated with taking his clients above tree line, and developed strategies to manage them, he is also realistic that there are some risks he can't manage or is unaware of altogether. Without complete knowledge or information, there is always some degree of exposure, and part of good decision making involves managing your risk tolerance. Fitzgerald has decided that continuing to Lion Head—and no farther—presents an acceptable level of risk for him and these two clients.

Before breaking tree line, the three add additional layers of clothing and gear in preparation for walking into the strong, sustained headwinds. As they work their way along the wind-battered, rocky trail, Fitzgerald regularly checks on his clients. When they arrive at Lion Head, they keep low to reduce the wind force as much as possible.

Fitzgerald will later recall the moment they arrive at their end point, where they shelter behind large boulders: "Winds from tree line were consistently at 50 mph. If we had stepped over Lion Head, I'm sure we would have gotten blasted by seventy-to-eighty-mile-per-hour winds. We didn't bother doing that. I told them at that point that we would not go above Lion Head."

In fact, Lion Head is a spot where "go or no-go" decisions get made all the time, sometimes to a hiker's detriment. Fitzgerald looks at his clients and says, "All right, guys, Lion Head. Let's go. Let's turn around." There is not a hint of resistance. The three turn back and, with the aid of the strong prevailing tailwind, make good time in getting to the shelter of tree line.

Mount Adams
1:20 p.m.

Although hiking downhill can often be as taxing or even more taxing on leg muscles than an uphill climb, it usually takes markedly less time. But as she did on Madison, Matrosova is again struggling with her descent from Adams. It has taken her thirty-three minutes to descend the same 159 vertical feet it took her forty minutes to ascend to reach her highest point. As she drives each heel of her boot into the fifty-degree slope, with 80-mph wind gusts pounding her back, she is desperately trying to keep from being blown over and sliding headfirst down the mountain. Nineteen minutes after she starts down, at 1:06 p.m., the Mount Washington Observatory records a wind gust of 105 mph.

Because of the winds and blowing snow, there is little visibility. Matrosova's handheld GPS is practically useless. If she were to hold it up in front of her face, it would be almost impossible to discern track or trail on the tiny screen. Because of this, she is inadvertently moving to the right of her original line of ascent, and at one point is 210 feet away from her original track up.

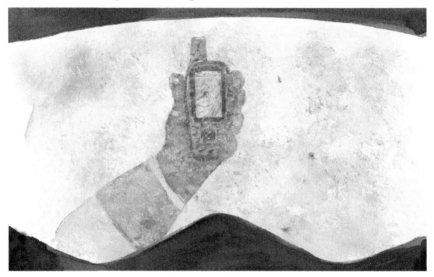

Shortly thereafter, she moves sharply to her left and closer to her earlier route of ascent. As she gets lower down on the slope, in addition to feeling the wind at her back, she is feeling its force from the side and even head on. Constantly and violently pummeled, she must be feeling dazed and exhausted. At 1:49 p.m., winds on Mount Washington are gusting to 86 mph, it is -17°F, and the windchill is -62°F.

At 1:54 p.m., Matrosova is now six feet from the original track she took to go up the mountain. It is possible her boot prints are invisible, having been erased by the wind. What happens next will eliminate any chance of her getting back on course and battling her way down toward Star Lake and Madison Hut. She walks alongside her original track for a short distance and then deviates significantly down and to the right, dropping into terrain that is loaded with deep snow, hidden boulders, and krummholz. She is essentially walking into what is known as a "terrain trap." Without snowshoes, she is post-holing in snows that are waist deep and higher.

It is possible that her goggles have frozen over, rendering them ineffective. Her neck gaiter, which was covered in frost when she took her selfie at Madison Hut, is by now frozen solid and forcing her exhalations upward and into her goggles, creating frost on the lenses in the arctic temperatures. In such a situation, taking your goggles off will exacerbate the problem, as your tears freeze, and then your eyes.

As her ground speed drops to almost zero, she is fully exposed and completely vulnerable to all the weather that is pouring into the area. When you're hiking—exhausted and disoriented—it is not uncommon to drop down as Matrosova is doing. Todd Johnstone-Wright, director of Wilderness Programs at Saint Michael's College in Colchester, Vt., has seen this happen firsthand. "You can watch someone hiking ahead of you, who's tired and unfamiliar with where they are, start to follow the contours of the terrain downward thinking it will provide the least resistance, when in fact, they don't realize they're actually getting further off trail," he said. "This is why lost hikers are often found down low in drainages."

As Matrosova continues through this terrain, she is on a direct line toward Star Lake but almost 130 feet below Star Lake Trail. There is no relief here. She must wallow through the thick blankets of snow.

Given what we know about the difficulty of making good decisions in complex situations while under duress, it is easy to appreciate the unmanageable number of complications Matrosova is experiencing at this moment. From a "human factors" standpoint, the list includes lack of adequate hydration and food; exhaustion; and the cognitive and physical impairments caused by the effects of hypothermia, which at this stage, are undeniable. She is also coping with environmental factors comprising extreme wind, frigid temperatures, deep snow, and low visibility, and physical factors that include krummholz, boulders, and the challenging terrain of the slope she's traversing.

As Matrosova gets closer to Madison Col, she is finding the winds even stronger. They are charging through this geological gap with the tremendous force of an attacking army. Meteorologist Ryan Knapp describes the force and pressure as the kind you experience when you "put your thumb over a garden hose." The winds here are as strong, if not stronger, than what she experienced higher up on the slopes of Adams.

Matrosova is foundering. She cannot rely on her past experience, because she hasn't encountered such conditions before. Neither can she fall back on her acquired skills and technical competency. She is unable to identify and execute a potential solution because she has reached a point where there isn't one. She has gone well beyond what the late, great alpinist Jean-Christophe Lafaille referred to as, "that narrow boundary between horror and joy." Lafaille himself ventured beyond that boundary on Makalu in 2006, and perished.

At 2:17 p.m., winds on Mount Washington are gusting to 96 mph, the temperature is -17°F, and the windchill is -64°F. Matrosova is barely holding on. It's impossible to know exactly when joy turned to horror for Matrosova, but at some point she emerged from the sweet dream of a great day in the mountains into the nightmare of a battle for survival.

AMC Pinkham Notch Parking Lot
Ammonoosuc Trailhead, Base Road
Mount Washington
3:00 p.m.

South of Matrosova, on opposite sides of Mount Washington, Thatcher and Mirkin, and Fitzgerald and Kilburn are arriving back at the trailheads where they started that morning. Their clients are tired, but it's a good tired. It has been a rewarding day out for all involved, and valuable lessons in decision making have been offered up. The four guides hope that, on the way home and over the coming days, their clients will reflect not only on the physical challenges they have encountered, but on the mental ones as well. They've had a good dose of Mother Nature's power, and they've learned that even experienced mountaineers have grown to respect it. They've also learned to accept that the summit will be there for them another day.

Below Star Lake Trail
Just before 3:15 p.m.

Matrosova has advanced 334 feet in an hour and twenty-three minutes, following a generally horizontal line on mostly sloped terrain. In all likelihood, she has been reduced to a crawl, pinned to the ground by the winds coming at her from all directions and from above. Fighting the winds, and the insubordination of her aching and lethargic muscles, she removes one of her arms from her backpack.

Grasping the zipper between her thumb and index finger, she opens the compartment on the pack's flap. This has to be difficult for her, given how cold it is. Fine motor skills go quickly in these temperatures. Moving her hand around the inside of the compartment, she finds her palm-size, hard plastic ResQLink personal locator beacon (PLB). She is probably holding both the beacon and the pack as firmly as she can manage so as not to lose them in the wind.

Finding the small clamp that holds the silver antenna in place around the body of the beacon, Matrosova pulls the antenna out of its hold. Somehow, in accordance with the instructions in the owner's manual and the illustration on the back of the beacon itself, she is able to position it in the palm of her hand with the faceplate pointed toward the sky, just as she learned to do a few days before. As she extends the beacon's antenna skyward, the flat aluminum antenna whips violently in the wind.

At an elevation of 4,875 feet, it has taken her two hours and twenty-eight minutes to descend 775 vertical feet to where she is now. She is just 135 feet from a place of familiarity, where she took her eight-minute pause some five hours before. She is a heartbreaking three-tenths of a mile from Madison Spring Hut, and another tenth of a mile from the safety of tree line.

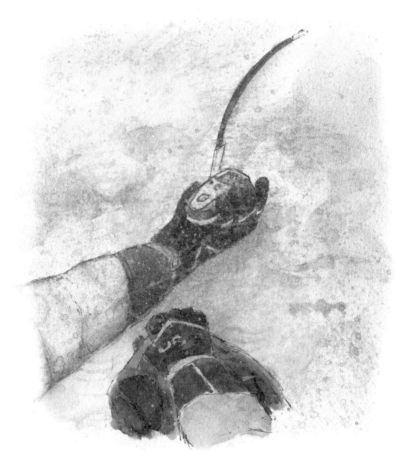

As she senses the approaching wave of unconsciousness, her vision narrowing, Matrosova is likely feeling darkness descend upon her. She depresses the small button on the side of the beacon. The opaque strobe on the faceplate of the beacon begins to flash. It's pulsing rhythmically, signaling that activation has been successful. She places the beacon back in her pack, where it will continue to flash and transmit data until it shuts down or is shut off.

The woman who, in a judo match, would choose to be "choked out" rather than to "tap out," is acknowledging defeat for the first and last time. At this moment, Mother Nature has achieved what Matrosova's judo opponents could not: her submission.

IX
RESISTANCE

"Death is the enemy. But the enemy has superior forces."

—*Atul Gawande , surgeon, author, and public health researcher*

Near Star Lake Trail
Approximately 3:20 p.m.

Somehow, amid the maelstrom of chaos and complications, Kate Matrosova succeeded once again in bending something to her will. She deployed her emergency beacon correctly, and managed to keep her ACR Electronics ResQLink 375's antenna vertical and the faceplate free of obstruction, thereby giving the Global Positioning System (GPS) "a clear view to the sky."

Capt. Bruce Determann, wing director of operations for the New Hampshire Civil Air Patrol, expressed surprise at Matrosova's ability to pull off this accomplishment, saying in an interview, "Given the extreme conditions, there's no way she should have been able to maintain proper position of the beacon long enough to get a signal. I think it's really fortunate that she held it correctly long enough to obtain a position. It's pretty remarkable, really."

Dr. Murray Hamlet says the kind of endurance Matrosova exhibited is not that surprising, given her internal motivation and drive. "We see huge differences in people's ability to do things in such conditions," he says. "You can't quantify how long even a deeply hypothermic person's motivation might drive them in those circumstances."

A GPS chip lies just beneath a beacon's faceplate. As Matrosova pressed the button to activate the beacon, the chip powered up and, acting as a receiver, began to search the sky for signals being transmitted by GPS satellites. When it was able to receive signals from three separate satellites, it triangulated and established longitude and latitude coordinates. Those coordinates then embedded into a 406.036 signal, and the beacon transitioned into a transmitter. The 406 signal, embedded with critical data, pinged skyward into orbit and was received by a geosynchronous satellite rotating at the same speed as the earth. Matrosova's beacon signal connected with satellite G13.

After G13 received the 406 signal, it transmitted the data to a Local User Terminal (LUT), from which the information was transmitted to a mission control center (MCC). In this case, the LUT and the MCC are located in the same place: Suitland, Md. The MCC is operated by the National Oceanic and Atmospheric Agency (NOAA).

Upon receiving the beacon's information, NOAA packaged it in a Keyhole Markup Zipped (KMZ) file, which included the coordinates and the owner's contact information, and sent the file electronically to the Air Force Rescue Coordination Center (AFRCC) at Tyndall Air Force Base in Lakeland, Fla. AFRCC is the agency with primary responsibility for coordinating all on-land search and rescue activities. Under a memorandum of understanding, the AFRCC delegates authority and execution for inland and woodland searches and rescues in New Hampshire to the state's Fish and Game Department.

AFRCC
Tyndall Air Force Base
Lakeland, Fla.
Approximately 3:20 p.m.

Staff Sgt. Bryan Turner is sitting at his monitoring station at the air base when he receives the KMZ file from NOAA. The activated beacon is registered to Kate Matrosova. Following protocol, Sgt. Turner calls Matrosova's cell phone number, the first on the contact list. The owner's phone is always the first to be called in case the beacon has been activated by accident. The call to Matrosova's phone immediately goes to voicemail. Turner then sends a text message to Matrosova, instructing her to "share your location with search and rescue."

His next phone call is to Farhoodi, the second person on the contact list. Farhoodi is in the couple's hotel room when his phone rings. Even before receiving the call, he is already concerned because he has watched the weather get progressively worse throughout the day. In fact, he's so worried that he visits the Mount Washington Observatory website and attempts to purchase expanded webcam access to the summit and surrounding peaks. But he is unable to do so because his credit card payment is too slow to process the purchase. Even if he were to gain access, he'd be unable to see beyond the lens of the summit cameras, which are now covered in thick frost because of the blowing snow and freezing conditions.

Staff Sgt. Turner advises Farhoodi of the beacon activation, and asks him if he is with Matrosova or knows where she is. Farhoodi informs him that she is out on a hike of the Northern Presidentials, and that if she has activated the beacon, she must be in really serious trouble. Turner collects some additional background detail from Farhoodi before ending the call. Immediately upon disconnecting, Farhoodi calls his wife's cell phone, but gets only the voicemail message.

At 3:33 p.m., Turner is on the phone with the New Hampshire State Police Dispatch Center in Twin Mountain to report the alert, and Dispatcher Garrett Stevens informs him that he is already aware of the situation and that New Hampshire Fish and Game will handle the emergency.

Route 302
Twin Mountain, N.H.
3:35 p.m.

Sgt. Mark Ober is finally clear of Northern Extremes Snowmobile Rentals, where he's just finished collecting information for his accident investigation. His 2012 Ford F250 cruiser is now pointed in the direction of home. But it won't be for long.

When Ober's cell phone rings, it's Dispatcher Stevens on the line. Stevens tells Ober that the AFRCC has received an emergency locator beacon activation near the summit of Mount Adams. Ober, who has participated in hundreds of missions as a member of his agency's search and rescue team, pulls his cruiser to the side of the road. The team was established in 1996 and is funded by a $1 fee assessed to boat, Off-Highway Recreational Vehicle, and ATV registrations, and through sales generated from the voluntary purchase of Hike Safe Cards.

Ober writes down the longitude and latitude coordinates recorded by the beacon's signal and contact information for Matrosova and Farhoodi. He then drives a short distance to the state-owned gas pumps and tops off his cruiser's tank—thirty gallons; it's been a busy shift. He decides to take advantage of the quiet location and good cell coverage to begin his work as incident commander. In a later interview, he will tell *Appalachia* journal writer Sandy Stott, "I hoped it was a mistake, an incidental activation by chance, because I knew where [the signal] was would be near impossible to get to today, tonight. I've had pretty good cell coverage there, so perhaps I could call and get in touch and find out."

Ober starts making calls. First, he reaches Turner at the AFRCC to gather additional information. He then calls Farhoodi, who tells him that he dropped off his wife at the Appalachia parking lot in Randolph at 5:00 a.m. that morning. Farhoodi describes his wife's itinerary, including the five peaks she was planning to summit along the Northern Presidential Traverse and her plan to be down at the Ammonoosuc Ravine trailhead for a 6:00 p.m. pickup on the Base Road.

Farhoodi tells Ober that Matrosova is an experienced mountaineer, having previously summited Denali, and that she is in very good physical condition. He adds that his wife wouldn't activate her beacon unless something serious was going on.

Farhoodi itemizes the clothing Matrosova is wearing and the gear and extra clothing she has brought with her. The list gives Ober pause, because he is hearing that Matrosova has packed light so she can move fast. She is not prepared to spend the night out on the range; she did not bring a tent, a bivy sack, or a sleeping bag, and she has no snowshoes. Ober asks if either Farhoodi or Matrosova checked the weather forecast before she set out. Farhoodi tells him that they did, but that she was determined to complete her goal.

After collecting as much information as he can about Matrosova's itinerary, equipment, and experience level, Ober continues making calls. He asks Dispatcher Stevens, who is now solely focused on this incident, to page three members of the Fish and Game Search and Rescue Team: Conservation Officers Matt Holmes, Glen Lucas, and Bob Mancini. He asks that they be instructed to call Ober back "Code 3," in law enforcement speak, the most exigent alert.

Stevens says he has been trying in vain to get an answer from Matrosova's cell and satellite phones. In New Hampshire, if you call 911 from your cell phone, a dispatcher will, in most circumstances, obtain your location coordinates almost immediately. While there are variables that can impact location accuracy, such as proximity of cell towers, an initial 911 call can give searchers a starting point. But in this case, Matrosova has not called 911, nor can anyone reach her on her cell phone in order to triangulate her location. The only option is to have her cell phone carrier "ping" her phone, so Ober asks Stevens to make that happen.

Ober then contacts Lt. Jim Kneeland, the assistant team leader of Fish and Game Search and Rescue (SAR). He explains to Kneeland what he knows of the situation and tells him he has already paged three members of the SAR team and plans to call them in. In a later interview, Ober will recall that Kneeland expresses some understandable concern about the mission. "I would be hesitant to send anyone up, but we should call [Col. Martin Garabedian] to find out," his lieutenant advises. Ober agrees, but says later, "It was bad out there, but I knew we were going."

Just after 4:00 p.m., Dispatcher Stevens calls Farhoodi to gather additional background information from him. Stevens later describes the interaction: "I felt terrible. I was telling him we were doing everything we could. I had only been on the job a year, and I was trying to comfort him as much as I could."

Meanwhile Ober continues to work his cell phone. After trying without success to reach the Mount Washington Observatory for a weather update, he contacts the most senior member of the law enforcement division of New Hampshire Fish and Game, Col. Martin Garabedian. As head of Fish and Game's law enforcement division, Garabedian is the person to make the final go or no-go call. Ober advises his colonel of the situation, and the two candidly discuss their options. They review current and forecasted weather conditions and the fact that the beacon coordinates are above tree line, and then decide who would be best to send on the mission.

Col. Garabedian tells Ober, "We have to try to get her," but stresses that he doesn't want rescuers to go above tree line to do so. He also instructs Ober to tell rescuers that if they feel at all uncomfortable, they should turn around and come down. "If they don't find her, get them out of there," he says.

Garabedian is adamant that he wants the decision about the extent of this night's mission to lie with those "at the tip of the spear." They will pull together a small group of rescuers and move them toward the last known beacon signal location. But they will go ahead only "as long as the weather supports the mission."

Reflecting on his decision that night, which was made from his home more than an hour's drive from the scene, Garabedian offers the following perspective: "Based on the information we had, there was nothing concrete as to whether [Matrosova] was above or below tree line. I wasn't going to put my personnel and the volunteers in harm's way, unless we knew exactly where she was, and then the question becomes whether we could have gotten to her without injuring ourselves."

Ober and Garabedian carefully review as many options as they can identify in order to arrive at a decision that aligns with the mission of the organization and the incident itself, while staying focused on minimizing the risk to search and rescue personnel. In doing this, they are working at a high level of situational awareness and risk evaluation, and are acknowledging their need to show humility in the face of conditions that could at some point outmatch their ability to manage them.

When asked how he cultivates a culture in which employees feel comfortable being candid with him about their concerns, Garabedian says, "I encourage push-back. I'm not going to hold it against them. People's lives are at risk here. I think any organization should do that. It doesn't matter if you're a CEO, a colonel, or a school superintendent—you need to have people you can trust to give you good information, both pro and con, so you can make the best possible decision." The fact that Garabedian encourages his people to tell truth to power minimizes one of the five factors of dysfunctional momentum—deference to perceived expertise—decreasing the likelihood that rescuers will feel pressured to push on when they feel the risk is too great.

After talking with his colonel, Ober calls Rick Wilcox. Since 1976, Wilcox has been president of the elite volunteer Mountain Rescue Service (MRS) based in Conway, N.H. He is an accomplished mountaineer who has summited several high peaks around the world, including Everest, and a renowned expert in search and rescue in the White Mountains. He is also known for having backed off numerous mountains because the conditions weren't favorable. MRS maintains a robust roster of the region's finest mountaineers. They are described as "world class" guides and climbers, and their level of technical competency and expertise is irrefutable.

Ober reviews with Wilcox the results of his discussion with Garabedian, including the colonel's decision to mount a rescue attempt. Wilcox tells Ober he will pull together a small team. In an interview with *Appalachia's* Sandy Stott, Ober says, "We defer to MRS in situations like this, more than people think. We ask for their advice and opinions on the safest way to conduct a rescue that is a life-or-death situation. They are the technical experts and are above tree line in the winter way more than we are."

At 4:09 p.m., still unable to get through to the Mount Washington Observatory, Ober asks Stevens to obtain current weather readings from summit personnel. Stevens soon reports that the current windchill on the peak is -30°F, winds out of the northwest are at 80 mph, and visibility is one-quarter mile. After several more calls, Ober heads to the Appalachia parking lot, where he will establish a command post.

Stevens is also busy on the phones and radio. His dispatch partner, Johnny Miller, handles all other incoming phone and radio traffic so his partner can continue to focus on managing the "Adams call."

Route 2 near Appalachia Parking Lot
Randolph, N.H.
Approximately 4:45 p.m.

Conservation Officer Matt Holmes is on his snow machine navigating the Presidential Rail Trail, having just cleared the snowmobile accident scene Ober sent him to earlier. It's just before dark, and the nine-year veteran of the New Hampshire Fish and Game Department Law Enforcement Division is returning to the Randolph Fire Department parking lot and the warmth of his cruiser, a 2012 Ford F250 three-quarter-ton pickup truck. He'll load the snow machine onto a trailer and head for home.

Holmes is cold, but he's in his element. As he has been for his entire career, he is responsible for a section of District 1, in the northern part of the state, which encompasses four towns and several unincorporated areas, including Sargent's Purchase, the home of the Northern Presidential Range. These unincorporated areas are remote regions with no infrastructure, except perhaps for the hundreds of mountain trails leading hikers to the summits. The town of Randolph, where the Appalachia trailhead is located just off Route 2, greets hikers in all seasons, all of them avid to reach at least one, if not all, of the summits along the Presidential Traverse.

"That is one of the busiest hiker hubs in my patrol," says Holmes of the trailhead. "If there's a lot of activity at Appalachia, there's a really good chance we're going to be called out for something. Holmes recalls looking up at the higher peaks of the Northern Presidentials on that Sunday, and making a quick assessment: "I could see just how hard the wind was pounding up there, thinking to myself, 'Boy, I'm glad I'm not up there.'"

As he has always done when he is on duty, day or night, whether on his snow machine or in his cruiser, Holmes heads over to the Appalachia parking lot to check it out. "I always cast my eyes on that parking lot to gauge whether or not I'm going to be called out that night," he says. "I distinctly remember when I came back through that there were no cars there. That fleeting moment was a huge relief." What Holmes doesn't know yet is that trouble is already in progress high up on the peak, and that Sgt. Ober is busy coordinating an intricate rescue effort and currently on his way to the empty parking lot that Holmes is about to leave.

Ober arrives at Appalachia just before 5:00 p.m. He, too, notes that the parking lot is empty, as it has been the two other times he's passed it that day on his way to and from the hospital. "Whew," he has said to himself each time he's passed by. "No one's up there. Good."

This time, he stops and parks his cruiser in front of the high snowbanks and establishes command in the same darkened parking lot that was illuminated by Matrosova's enthusiasm and headlamp some twelve hours earlier. Using his iPhone as a "hotspot," he is able to establish an internet connection for his laptop computer. He checks "Summit Conditions" on the Mount Washington Observatory website. The data is grim: -37°F and winds exceeding 100 mph. By this time, the weather has churned into a full-blown tempest in the upper atmosphere and is making its way down into the valley. Ober feels his cruiser being rocked by the strong gusts of wind and notes down a temperature of -10°F.

As search and rescue team members are notified, and he awaits their arrival, Ober sits in his cruiser and continues taking and making a steady stream of phone calls. He's on the phone with Dispatcher Stevens at Troop F, the AFRCC's Turner, Col. Garabedian, Lt. Jim Goss, and Rick Wilcox. Stevens, who has been working the cell and satellite phone components of the operation, explains to Ober that the satellite phone carrier has pinged Matrosova's phone, but because it is turned off or its battery has died, they cannot get a location. They report that the phone has not been turned on since Feb. 12, three days earlier.

Meanwhile, according to Stevens "there must be exigent circumstances, like a life or death situation," before a cell phone carrier is allowed to ping a phone. After submitting the necessary form to the carrier, Stevens learns that the last known location of the cell was recorded at 11:30 a.m. that day in North Conway, clearly a false reading. "In the mountains, you don't get good readings because coverage isn't great," he says. The information does indicate that Matrosova's cell phone was on at 11:30 a.m. that day, when she was mid-slope on her way up Mount Adams. Whether she was checking for cell coverage or a weather update or trying to make a call remains a mystery, but we do know that this is the last time the phone was detected by a cell tower.

At 5:00 p.m., Ober receives notification from AFRCC of an updated beacon location sent from Matrosova's device. He again uses his cell phone to establish a hot spot for his laptop and enters the new coordinates. It is not uncommon for a conservation officer, during the busy summer hiking season, to sit at his kitchen table with his laptop computer in the middle of the night and work with lost hikers to determine their coordinates, and then calmly and supportively talk them to the closest trailhead. If only it were July.

According to the new coordinates, Matrosova is now on the north side of Mount Madison, which faces Ober's location. She is located approximately six-tenths of a mile southeast of the original beacon hit, between the Valley Way and Watson Path. This new information provides a strong dose of optimism for Ober. If it is accurate, Matrosova is moving and has gotten herself below tree line. In that case, her chances of self-rescuing or being rescued have improved significantly, as has the safety of the soon-to-be-deployed rescuers.

"I felt relief," recalls Ober. "I saw where she was, and she was not on the ridge. She was off trail but down fairly low. I thought, 'That's great. We're going to get her. It will be a while, but if she keeps moving down, the guys will pick up her tracks and get her.' That was a good feeling."

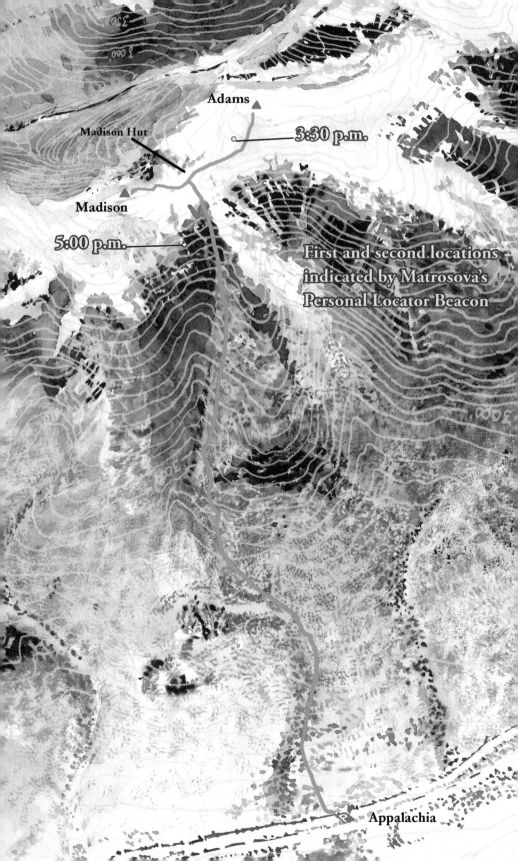

Adams

Madison Hut

3:30 p.m.

Madison

5:00 p.m.

First and second locations
indicated by Matrosova's
Personal Locator Beacon

Appalachia

It's now around 5:15 p.m., and Holmes is in the Randolph Fire Department parking lot, securing his snow machine onto his trailer, when he receives a radio call from Ober. "Bring your search and rescue gear," Ober says. "There's an incident on Mount Adams. We need to go up there."

Holmes is incredulous, having just passed an empty Appalachia parking lot. "Are you serious?" he replies. Sitting in his idling cruiser, Holmes takes another assessment of the situation around him: "The summits are locked in, the wind is absolutely howling, even in the trees. They're going to be exponentially worse up there," he recalls thinking. "The cold and bad weather had been a staple on the news a couple of days leading up to that event. It was a mainstream story that the weather was going to get bad over the next few days. We'll generally see a downturn of activity during those types of weather events. People will head home prior to the event."

Holmes acknowledges that his first reaction to Ober's news was anger. "The weather had been predicted well in advance," he says. "This was a storm that shouldn't have snuck up on somebody. But as often happens, the worst part of a rescue is the first step out of bed, out the door, out of the truck, to start the whole event. Once it starts, you're fully committed. Feeling the sting of the weather, you also feel for the victim. I know how much it's hurting me, but it's hurting them far worse, and I want to relieve them of that." Sure enough, as the rescue attempt evolved, says Holmes, "my temperament softened toward Kate and her situation."

Sunset from the summit of Mount Washington on Feb. 15, 2015. If all had gone as planned, Kate Matrosova would by now be below tree line on the Ammonoosuc Ravine Trail, and less than one hour from being met by her husband at the Ammonoosuc Ravine parking area.

Immediately after speaking with Ober, Holmes resigns himself to the inevitable, makes the short drive into Gorham, and purchases food to keep him fueled during the long, grueling hours to come. As he drives back to the fire department to gear up, he calls his wife. "It's brutally cold, so it's not going to be a good rescue scenario," he tells her. After nine years of such phone calls, his wife knows the drill. "Be careful," she says, not realizing it will be another ten hours before they see each other.

Littleton, N.H.
Approximately 5:15 p.m.

Conservation Officer Bob Mancini is on his department-issued snow machine, and he's uncomfortably cold. It is -14°F, and Mancini's eyes are bothering him. "The snow machine mask I was wearing under my helmet wasn't doing the job, so my face was cold," he says in an interview. Mancini, a five-year veteran of Fish and Game and a member of the search and rescue (SAR) team, is on his way to meet up with his friend and partner, Conservation Officer Glen Lucas, another member of the SAR team, at the Moore Dam Reservoir boat launch. They're planning to patrol the network of local trails for as long as they can tolerate the conditions. Maybe they'll discover a snowmobiler who has broken down somewhere or stumble into one of those incidents you encounter in law enforcement that you can't make up.

As he listens to his portable radio, Mancini overhears Ober instructing Holmes to grab his gear and prepare for a rescue mission on Adams. Mancini, a veteran who served in the National Guard as a military policeman for six years, retrieves his cell phone and calls Ober to ask if he will be needed. Ober tells him he will indeed be needed. And when he learns that Lucas is nearby, he tells Mancini to ask Lucas to gear up as well and that both should report to the Randolph Fire Department. Mancini, ten miles of flat ground away from his cruiser, turns his sled around and heads back to it, thinking, "This is going to be a long night. This is going to be really tough."

Arriving at his cruiser, Mancini loads his sled onto the trailer and makes haste to the reservoir to meet Lucas. Meanwhile, the extreme cold is having an impact. Lucas recalls that when he set out on his patrol that afternoon, he was wearing "extreme-winter boots," and that everything "was on high on my sled—hand and foot warmers—and I was still cold."

Why are Lucas and Mancini even out in this weather? It has everything to do with the rest of us. They have sworn to protect us, and sometimes that means protecting us from ourselves—and our misguided decisions. They're out on snow machines in arctic temperatures in case we get ourselves into trouble, or find it on our way, and require their intervention.

Mancini arrives at the boat launch and fills in Lucas. "You're kidding me?" Lucas recalls thinking. "I don't want to go up in this." But he soon shifts to more practical concerns: "Where's my stuff? What am I bringing?" The two load Lucas's sled onto Mancini's trailer and make a fast drive to Lucas's house, where he can gear up.

Lucas's wife is surprised to see him home so soon, and he explains that he's on his way back out for a search and rescue call on Mount Adams. Though they live west of the Presidential Range, she is well aware of the extreme weather conditions, because by now they are making their presence felt throughout the region. "I really don't want you to go," she says. Her wary reaction is understandable, but it's matched by the deeper knowledge that her husband could be going on a lifesaving mission and needs to be up there. So, as Lucas gathers and double-checks everything in his SAR pack, his wife prepares hot fluids and food to help him through what she fears will be a long and difficult night.

Mancini, with his SAR gear already in the back of his truck, is on the phone with his wife as he drives to Randolph. "My wife is my best support system," he says. "If she knows I'm going out on a call such as this, she'll boil water, and pack snacks for me, and tell me, 'Just be safe.'" But he doesn't have the time to stop at home this time, and his wife is extra concerned. "You're going out in this?" she asks. He confirms what they both know is obvious. "Just be careful, don't do anything stupid, and come home safe," she tells him.

Randolph Fire Department
Randolph, N.H.
Approximately 6:00 p.m.

As Holmes prepares his gear, he is joined by Mancini and then Lucas. These three know one another well. They often work shifts and calls together, have trained together, and over time have become good friends. As they all don protective gear, they chat about the forthcoming mission. Lucas recalls, "We had a good talk, making sure we all had gear, acknowledging to one another, 'This is no joke.' It was all-business talk." Like the band of brothers they have become, they take time and care making sure each of them is fully equipped and prepared for what's ahead. "We were taking inventory, bouncing ideas off of each other, making sure we had the appropriate gear," Holmes recalls. "If you don't have it with you when you go in, you're not going to get it. I repack for every single mission I go on. Always."

Holmes fills a Nalgene water bottle with warm tap water, and also brings cold fluids because he finds he hydrates better if he has both available. Mancini has an almost clinical method of gearing up. "I pack every piece of equipment I have," he says. "A stove, food and water, gear to spend the night, water purification tablets, fire starter, rudimentary items for anything from first aid to gear repair, a tourniquet, and a Norwegian heater." A Norwegian heater is a portable stove that essentially acts as a small furnace that can keep you warm. "Everything is compartmentalized in specific color-coded bags that I carry in two totes," adds Mancini. "It's just more efficient." His "Oh, shit bag," packed for emergencies, is orange.

As they prepare, they stress to each other the importance of speaking up if one of them is uncomfortable with what's going on or doesn't feel good. Each knows he is heading into a very difficult situation, and they repeat to each other that if they are to go on to search and rescue another day, their own safety is paramount.

Appalachia Parking Lot
6:30 p.m.

Some people harbor the misconception that if they send out a call for help in the backcountry, aid will arrive as quickly as an ambulance in an urban environment. That is simply not the case. As Ober will explain to writer Sandy Stott, "It's the calling. Getting a rescue together takes a lot of calling. And that calling takes a lot of time." Fish and Game search and rescue personnel have other assignments as well, including regular patrol duties. Or they may be off duty and have to gear up and respond from various parts of the state. Volunteer rescuers must juggle their jobs and other responsibilities in order to prepare for and respond to a call. Mike Cherim, a member of the Androscoggin Valley Search and Rescue (AVSAR) Team, tells Stott, "It takes a long time for help to come. Be prepared to help yourself. Expecting or anticipating a timely rescue when the need arises is foolhardy."

That advice is borne out today as Holmes, Lucas, and Mancini arrive at the command post at Appalachia to meet with Ober a full three hours after Matrosova's locator beacon emits its first signal. It will take at least another three hours for them to ascend to the area where she is believed to be. The team is carrying enough gear for self-care and additional protective clothing, food, and shelter for Matrosova.

Ober briefs them on the plan he, Col. Garabedian, and Rick Wilcox have developed: Mancini, Holmes, and Lucas will take snow machines as far up the Valley Way as possible, then hike to a point on the trail that lies about 1,000 yards southwest, across the valley from and parallel to the location of the second beacon hit near Pine Link Trail. Once there, they will await the team members from Mountain Rescue Service, who are at present gearing up and on their way to the Appalachia parking lot. Ober tells the three rescuers that they are not to go above tree line, nor are they to drop down into the steep, treacherous drainage that separates the Valley Way from the spot near the Pine Link Trail that is the location of the second beacon signal. Ober loads the coordinates of the second beacon hit into Mancini's handheld GPS so the three will know when they have arrived at the spot across the valley from it, and orders them "to take no unnecessary risks." He exhorts them to turn around if they feel their lives are in danger at any point.

As conditions on the summit of Mount Washington and the surrounding peaks continue to deteriorate, Mancini, Holmes, and Lucas make last-minute preparations and unload snowmobiles from the trailer. At 6:39 p.m., they are ready to start riding up the Valley Way. While the hiking trail remains discernable, there is still deep snow beyond the hikers' trough, so they have to break trail as they ride. It takes them thirty minutes to get a half-mile in. "We kept getting stuck, taking routes around fallen trees," Holmes recalls. "But it was a worthwhile effort, because we were each carrying seventy-five-to-eighty-pound packs." Lucas recalls a silver lining to the tough ride. "It was kind of nice getting the sleds unstuck; it got us warmed up," he says.

The three make it to the first junction of the trail, before it pitches to the right, and then stop. Once they determine they can take the sleds no farther, they shut them down, don their heavy packs, and start hiking up the trail. They do not need snowshoes yet, but they have them strapped onto their packs.

Thinking back on the moment, Holmes says, "We started hiking. All business. We talked at the beginning, but as the hike wore on the talk slowed." Lucas remembers being cold. "You always start cold," he says. "But I never warmed up to the point of comfort. I started out with just a base layer. I should have had a mid-layer on. It was my own fault." Mancini recalls similar challenges with layering. "I didn't change my socks at the fire station," he admits. "I should have. It still pisses me off to this day. My feet got very cold, so cold up top I didn't even want to change my socks. I should have done a complete strip-down to remove the moisture." Even Holmes says he had trouble with thermoregulation, finding it difficult to arrive at the optimal combination of clothing to stay warm but not sweat too much.

So, as careful and thoughtful as they have been about preparing for a cold, grueling outing, they still find themselves at the mercy of the conditions they are encountering along the way and in need of adapting their behavior to those conditions if they hope to succeed.

As they ascend on foot, they find the snow packed down hard with no loose powder, so the going is not too difficult, and they still don't feel the need to put on snowshoes. As they move up, their thoughts begin to turn to the woman they have been called to rescue. Mancini recalls, "We knew she was in really bad shape. It was life threatening. I thought she was barely hanging on or had expired. We hoped barely hanging on. The position had changed, and it looked like she was moving down. We were really excited. We'd be able to get her warmed up with the Norwegian heater and a hypo-wrap. We were psyched, and we had to get there."

As is often the case on a mountain rescue mission, these three are gaining momentum from hope. If they can imagine a happy ending, it helps them to keep going. "We really wanted to get to the second beacon hit," says Holmes. "We were relatively confident we could get to it. We thought there might be a chance if we found her at the second beacon. Maybe she was below the trees in a sleeping bag. In that case it would be a survivable incident." Still, there is a nagging worry because, as they all know in the moment and Holmes will articulate later, "There was just no way to survive up on that ridge."

At some point, as Holmes and Mancini are moving ahead with haste and optimism, Lucas starts to slow and enters a state of physical decline. The cold stays with him; he just can't shake it off. He feels himself falling behind, and recognizes that there's still a long way to go and a longer night ahead. "My body just started to fail," he recalls sadly. "My quads were tightening up to the point where I was stiff-legged. I kept pushing and pushing myself."

Meanwhile, Mancini is on a mission to get to Matrosova, and his single-minded drive creates a gap between him and his teammates. "I didn't realize how far behind me they were, because I was going pretty fast," he says. "That was a mistake on my part. I just wanted to get there, and I failed to stay with my buddies."

Lucas is getting worse, and when Holmes takes note of his friend's struggle, he begins to walk back to him. Mancini then realizes he has lost sight of his teammates and also turns back.

Lucas is aware that his predicament is having an impact on the mission. "I'm a liability to my teammates," he says of the situation. "If I continue, the rescue will be for me and not this woman."

As the three discuss next steps, Lucas girds himself to be candid. "I'm going to man up and swallow my pride here, guys," he tells his friends. "I can't do this." He says he was embarrassed at the time but adds, "I felt comfortable saying I couldn't go, but I think if I was a new guy, I might have continued to push."

Mancini and Holmes do not want to leave Lucas there alone, but he is persistent and tells them he'll be fine once he warms up in his bivy sack. Hypothermia is knocking on his door, and exhaustion is already in the house. Lucas feels he just needs to take back control, and he'll be okay. They agree that Holmes will help Lucas get into his bivy sack, and Mancini will continue up the trail.

When Lucas tries by himself to handle the task of getting in his portable shelter, he is unable to do it. "My fingers wouldn't work," he recalls. "I had my hand warmers in the zippered chest pocket on my insulated bibs, and I couldn't physically open the zipper." Seeing that his friend's fine motor skills are shot, Holmes opens the pocket for him. "I felt like a child," Lucas says. Reflecting on that feeling, Lucas highlights the importance of humility in making solid judgment calls. "It's tough for us to admit [anything less] when we're expected to be the best," he says.

Holmes and Mancini also show great judgment in empathizing with Lucas's predicament and supporting his need to care for himself before he himself becomes a rescue mission. "It wasn't working for him at that point," says Holmes. "We weren't going to push him."

Holmes retrieves the bivy sack from Lucas's backpack and gets him inside. He then activates several hand warmers and places them inside Lucas's down parka and on his legs. He ensures his friend is as insulated as he can be, and again says he doesn't want to leave him. Lucas tells him he'll be okay, and urges him to continue the mission. Holmes radios Ober that Lucas is stopping, that he is all right, and that he and Mancini will continue up. As Lucas lies there beside the trail, some 2.75 miles from the Appalachia trailhead below, he watches the glow of his friend's headlamp disappear into the darkness ahead and turns to the work of getting himself warm.

Appalachia Parking Lot
Approximately 7:30 p.m.

As Mancini and Holmes continue upward, and Lucas wages a personal battle trailside, members of Mountain Rescue Service (MRS) start arriving at the trailhead and check in with Ober. Steve Dupuis, Geoff Wilson, Scott Lee, and Steve Larson already know what they're getting themselves into, having been briefed by Wilcox when he phoned them in. Ober loads the coordinates of the second beacon hit into Wilson's GPS unit, as he did with Mancini's, and they all agree that, with Dupuis as team leader, the four rescuers will ascend the Valley Way and rendezvous with the conservation officers who are already on the trail.

Dupuis (who will take over from Rick Wilcox as president of MRS in 2016), assures Ober that his team will do everything they can to reach the second beacon site, but that they will take no unnecessary risks. He and Ober agree that if the second beacon hit yields no results, the MRS team will assess the situation and decide if going above tree line is an option—but that seems highly unlikely at this point.

Ober says Dupuis believes that if Matrosova has made it to the location of the second beacon hit, she will be unable to go much farther because she will have encountered waist-deep snow and is without snowshoes. Later, Dupuis will explain his thinking at the time in an interview with Chris Jensen of New Hampshire Public Radio: "People survive some incredible things. I'm just hoping for the best, that she's found a hole to dig into, to get out of the wind."

Putting the MRS team in charge of decision making at tree line is a sign of Ober's respect for Dupuis's judgment. "I trust him implicitly," he says. For his part, Mancini describes Dupuis as "a mountain man," adding, "He's tough as nails. He's professional and more knowledgeable than anyone I know. He's a role model for me, and a good communicator—very, very capable. When Steve is involved, it makes everyone a better player. He knows people's strengths and weaknesses, and leverages their strengths. There's a quiet confidence there."

The trust that Ober and Mancini place in Dupuis's judgment and Lucas's willingness to speak the truth about his difficulties to his teammates on the Valley Way are strong examples of the elements involved in "team psychological safety," a term used by Dr. Michael Roberto, trustee professor of management at Bryant University, in his 2002 case study of the 1996 Mount Everest disaster. In fact, all the search and rescue groups that will converge, by land or by air, on the Northern Presidential Range over the next several hours will demonstrate good skills in acting responsibly and safely as team members.

Roberto defines team psychological safety as the "shared belief that the team is safe for interpersonal risk taking" (Edmondson, *Administrative Science Quarterly*, 1999). "Team members demonstrate a high level of trust and mutual respect for one another," he writes. "[They] do not believe that the group will rebuke, marginalize, or penalize individuals for speaking up or challenging prevailing opinions."

According to Roberto, there are three conditions that drive group or team behavior and decision making: 1) member status differences; 2) leader coaching and support; and, 3) level of familiarity or prior interaction. It is normal for us to size up others within our group, establishing status differences. This kind of scorekeeping causes us to label others and make assumptions about levels of experience and expertise, and it can contribute to the construction of perceived hierarchies within the group. These instinctual reactions can sometimes help group members to recognize each others' strengths and weaknesses before activities commence, but they can also create a barrier to establishing an environment of transparency and trust. When members of a group or team perceive their own status as less than that of others, they are much less apt to express concerns out of fear of isolating themselves or projecting personal weakness.

When there is a clear group or team leader, that individual's leadership will have a tremendous impact on how the team will behave. There is not a one-size-fits-all leadership style for every situation or activity. But leadership behavior sets a tone, and it can be positive or negative.

Finally, familiarity with others in the group or team can work in one of two ways. Lack of familiarity can make members insecure and hesitant to be truthful and trusting. On the other hand, a strong sense of familiarity can lead to overconfidence or complacency, particularly when there's been a high level of success during prior activities.

Team members must be aware of all these factors when they engage in a group activity, especially one that carries a degree of risk. A lack of psychological safety creates an environment in which individuals will not speak up, even when they are uncomfortable with or unable to manage the system they are in. "An absence of candid discussion and constructive dissent makes it difficult to identify and solve problems before they trigger a series of other breakdowns in the system," writes Roberto.

When respected and embraced, the three components of team psychological safety not only mitigate risk but can also be the keys to a successful outcome. In this case, of course, a successful outcome includes locating Matrosova. But those in charge of the search and rescue operation must also keep all team members safe from start to finish. That means giving them permission to speak up if they feel uncomfortable with the situation or unable to manage it safely. And it means helping them trust each other and their leaders as they embark on a high-risk activity. Thus far, the leaders involved in the search for Matrosova are exhibiting all the qualities that lead to team psychological safety, and that will continue throughout the entire operation.

Just after 7:30 p.m., having been updated on the plans for the rescue mission by Dispatcher Stevens, and holding out hope, Charlie Farhoodi sends his wife a text message. He sends his love, informs her that the rescuers are coming for her using the same route she hiked in on, and offers words of encouragement. The text goes unanswered.

At approximately 7:45 p.m., as the four MRS rescuers are making final preparations to leave, Ober receives a third set of coordinates from the AFRCC. When he enters this new set of coordinates into the laptop's software program, the news is not good at all. According to the coordinates, Matrosova is now in the middle of King Ravine, almost a mile northwest of the second beacon hit. "This really threw us for a loop," Ober will say later. King Ravine is a massive, glacially inflicted scar on the northwest side of Mount Adams. In winter, with heavy snowloads, it is highly prone to avalanches. Even in daylight and in good winter conditions, it is high-risk territory. At night during a snowstorm, it is treacherous. "There's no way we're going to King Ravine," Ober recalls thinking. "It can't happen. People will die." The news dampens the optimism that has been fueled by the hope that they will find Matrosova at the second beacon hit.

Now, things are looking strange. With three different locator beacon sites, there is no way to know what information is reliable. Ober decides to stick with the plan they have in place. So, with the second beacon site on their radar, the MRS team climbs over the snowbank and starts up the Valley Way.

The Valley Way
Approximately 8:00 p.m.

Glen Lucas is lying on the ground, his arms wrapped tightly around him to hold in warmth, on the side of the trail where Holmes and Mancini left him about twenty minutes earlier. Even though he's wearing all his gear, is stuffed in a bivy sack, and has hand warmers strategically placed on his body, he's not getting warmer. He is in the early stages of hypothermia, and if he doesn't do something, his situation will turn critical. "I'm lying in my bag, and it isn't getting any better," he will say later. "I was freezing cold. I was scared. I knew I had to move. I knew I was shutting down." An eight-year veteran of Fish and Game, and a six-year member of the SAR team, he knows what is happening to him but still experiences it as surreal. "If I fall asleep, this is how I find people, dead in a bivy sack against a tree," he thinks. "I need to move, and I need to move now." So Lucas wills himself to stand up, gather his gear, and start back down the trail toward Appalachia.

Higher up on the trail, Mancini is the first to arrive at the staging point where he and Holmes are meant to rendezvous with the MRS team. It's brutally cold up there. As he waits for Holmes, he takes immediate steps to maintain body warmth. "I'm doing jumping jacks; I'm walking up and down the trail forty feet, pacing back and forth," he recalls. "It's working, but not well enough."

So Mancini takes his Jetboil stove and a fuel canister out of his backpack but finds that the fuel he needs to light his stove is frozen and useless. His exposed hands are also freezing as he tries to manipulate his gear. He grabs his insulated pants and parka from the pack and puts them on. He adds glove liners and mountaineering mittens and swaps out his sweat-drenched hat. All this makes a difference, at least for the moment.

"It was weird," he says as he conjures the weather he was in. "The wind was always steady, but every once in a while, Mother Nature would unleash her wrath. It was a deafening sound through the ridge. Just above us, where the wind was like ninety to a hundred, it was like a freight train coming through. The wind didn't bother me; it was the cold. I've been in terrible, direct headwinds on Mount Washington, and while I wasn't in direct headwinds on the trail, the cold was unbearable."

Holmes arrives as Mancini is adding layers of clothing, and they try to beat back the cold as they wait for MRS. "We were pacing on the trail," he says. "We had on every piece of gear, including our down jackets, and it was still very cold. If something went bad for us, our only option was to dig a snow shelter, and bivy up."

They continue to try to light the stove. As they retrieve gear from one another's packs, they are finding it difficult to make their hands work. "We were both shivering hard," says Holmes. "We'd each go into a pack wearing a glove liner until we couldn't feel our hands, then swap off for the next person to retrieve items." They want to get the stove running so that, when the MRS rescuers arrive, everyone can have the benefit of hot liquids or Jell-o. Holmes finally locates one of his larger fuel canisters and finds it has yet to freeze. The winds are blowing so hard through the trees that Mancini needs to dig a pit in the deep snow so they can get the stove out of the wind to light it.

Once they are able to light the stove, it gets warmer, and they are able to cook hot Jell-o. "It was a real morale booster," says Mancini. "I was in bad shape about twenty minutes before. I was mildly hypothermic."

Appalachia Parking Lot
Between 8:00 and 10:00 p.m.

As he has all night, Mark Ober continues to work the phones. He calls Rick Wilcox to ask for a second MRS team that can carry a rescue litter up the trail. He talks with the New Hampshire Air National Guard to see if they can have a Blackhawk helicopter crew on standby for the following morning, and he contacts New Hampshire Civil Air Patrol to see if an airplane with beacon tracking capability will be available as well.

Ober also calls Bill Arnold of the Androscoggin Valley Search and Rescue (AVSAR) Team. Like MRS, the AVSAR Team is made up of volunteers, some of whom are both "Winter Above Tree line" and "Winter Below Tree line" qualified. Founded in 1993, the team participates in numerous backcountry search and rescue operations in the Whites in all seasons. Ober asks Arnold to put out a call for team members to be on standby in the event Matrosova isn't located that night, and they need to resume the search the next morning. Arnold immediately records the following message and sends it out to members of the winter team's registered phone numbers:

This is an AVSAR call. This is Bill Arnold calling from AVSAR, at about 8:30 p.m. on Sunday, February 15th. We have an overdue hiker, who apparently has set off her personal beacon somewhere on the north slope of either Mount Madison or Mount Adams. Fish and Game is having a hard time figuring that out. They have sent up a group from Fish and Game and one from MRS to try to locate this woman, but they're putting together groups to go out tomorrow morning, Monday, to search for her. The plan is to meet at Appalachia at 8:00 a.m. If you're available, please give me a call.

Throughout the Mount Washington Valley, cell and home phones ring to life, as AVSAR members get the news. The members who will sign on to participate that night include both veterans and newbies.

For Matt Bowman, who's spending a quiet evening at home with his wife when he gets the call, this will be at least his fiftieth SAR response. For Brett and Corey Fitzgerald and Erik Thatcher, this will be their first.

In fact, Brett and Corey have yet to be officially named to the "Winter Above Tree Line Team." They haven't completed their "shakedown" qualifying hike. Brett will say later, "I don't think they intended to call us." But the brothers are known as excellent guides and are well respected in the climbing community. If Matrosova is not found that night, a lot of rescue power will be needed the next day, and the Fitzgerald brothers have the skills to help.

Ober continues making contingency plans with Col. Garabedian, Lt. Jim Goss, and Lt. Wayne Saunders. Goss and Saunders will respond the next morning if that night's search is unsuccessful. "We're thinking that hopefully we find her," says Garabedian. "But we're making a contingency plan [in case] we're not going to, so we start planning for the next day. We've learned the importance of this the hard way."

The Valley Way
Between 8:39 p.m. and 11:00 p.m.

As Dupuis and his MRS team ascend the trail, they are mindful of their pace, moving with urgency but also careful not to sweat so as to avoid freezing when they stop. "You have to take the slow-and-steady approach and plod along," he will say to New Hampshire Public Radio's Chris Jensen. "It is quite a conundrum."

Along the route, they encounter Lucas making his way down. Lucas fondly recalls the greeting he receives from Dupuis. "I love Steve. He says to me, 'Dude, are you all right?' I could tell he knew I wasn't doing well." They talk briefly, and after Lucas assures the team he is all right, the four continue upward, while Lucas keeps castigating himself. "I felt like I failed the mission," he says. In fact, he's using excellent judgment and practicing self-care so that others are spared the task of caring for him, which would take focus and energy away from their main rescue effort.

Back at the Appalachia parking lot, Ober is dealing with his own adversity. Between 8:39 p.m. and 10:19 p.m., AFRCC sends him three more hits from Matrosova's locator beacon. Now he has a grand total of six. The most recent hit shows the beacon to be in the Great Gulf Region off the Osgood Trail approximately 1.75 miles from beacon hit number two. This is on the far side of Mount Madison from the Valley Way trailhead. At 9:26 p.m., a second new hit targets the same location. Then at 10:19 p.m., a third hit seems to be targeting King Ravine again, at a spot approximately 600 feet northwest of the King Ravine Trail. Clearly, the six hits can't all be accurate, and Ober is at a loss. In his *Appalachia* journal essay, "Looking for Kate," Sandy Stott captures the moment perfectly when he writes that "tech complexity morphed into perplexity."

At 10:28 p.m., Charlie Farhoodi places a call to Dispatcher Stevens looking for an update. "He called a few times," says Stevens. "He was upset. He was really confused about everything that was going on. He felt helpless because he couldn't go up there and help her."

After a slow, painful descent, Lucas finally walks out of the woods and into the Appalachia parking lot at 10:45 p.m. He walks over to Ober and immediately apologizes. "I don't feel right," he says, and Ober responds with a reassuring acknowledgment that "it's terrible out there." When Lucas gets to his truck, he coaxes himself inside and takes a series of photographs of himself so he can see what he looks like. In fact, he looks exactly like he feels: beaten up. The photos reveal a guy who is very cold, exhausted—and deeply disappointed. He starts the motor to bring warmth into the truck and readies himself to wait for his two friends to come back down.

Conservation Officer Glen Lucas, cold and exhausted,
photographs himself shortly after returning to his cruiser
following his ordeal on the Valley Way.

Just before 11:00 p.m. the second MRS team, designated MRS2, arrives with a rescue litter. Team members Bayard Russell, Max Lurie, Nick Aiello, and Janet Wilkinson listen to Ober's briefing and prepare to ascend the Valley Way towing the litter in the event Matrosova is found or a rescuer is stricken.

As the four prepare to depart, Charlie Farhoodi approaches them in the parking lot. In an interview with Stott, Wilkinson says, "He was gentle and kind and appreciative of our being there. I was surprised that he didn't seem more panicked." Perhaps Farhoodi's confidence in his wife's ability to succeed at anything she tries is holding up for the time being, though his unexpected presence at the trailhead certainly reveals a high level of concern.

The Valley Way
After 11:00 p.m.

Sometime between 11:00 and 11:30 p.m., the first four MRS rescuers arrive at the staging point where Holmes and Mancini have been trying desperately to stay warm, and the six of them review the situation. At this point, Dupuis is in charge of decision making. When he realizes the negative effect the cold is having on Holmes and Mancini, he tells them they should go down rather than accompany the MRS team into the drainage that will lead to the second locator beacon hit. "I told [Dupuis] I respected him and that I always listened to him," says Mancini, "but I wasn't going to let them go into the woods without anyone there." So they strike a compromise: the MRS team will move down and across to the second beacon hit, while Holmes and Mancini will stay put and coordinate a rescue if one or more of the team gets into trouble.

Conservation Officer Bob Mancini confers with two members of Mountain Rescue Service at the staging area high on the Valley Way.

They also decide that there is no way anyone is going above tree line toward the first beacon hit, because it would be a "suicide mission," says Holmes. "It was just flat out not conducive to life."

The MRS team decides to hike toward the second beacon hit location for forty minutes. If they are unable to get there in that time, they will turn around and come back to the staging area. The four leave the familiarity of the Valley Way and carefully descend the steep slope leading into the drainage.

Later, in a much warmer setting, Dupuis will describe the tough going to NHPR's Jensen: "You go into a pocket, and you may slip down two or three feet deeper than you thought. The snow could be ten or twelve feet deep in there because of the way a tree held up the snow. And you are almost walking on top of some of the small trees."

The four are wearing headlamps with remote batteries nestled against their bodies so they won't drain in the cold. Though they are below tree line, Dupuis guesses the wind at 90 mph. "There were times when it was difficult to stand and other times when there was a little bit of a lull and we were fine," he said to Jensen. "But it was raging pretty hard. When your nostrils freeze together it is pretty darn cold." The walls of fir trees are also presenting a risk. "You can be stopped dead in your tracks [by one]," said Dupuis.

In his article headlined "The young woman and the mountain" (Feb. 22, 2015), *Boston Globe* reporter Nestor Ramos writes that "as they neared the location of Matrosova's second beacon reading, the hike turned into a crawl. Off the packed trail, the men forced their way through snow that reached their chests despite their snowshoes, hacking their way through brush."

Just before 1:00 a.m., the MRS team arrives at the location of the second beacon, and the four rescuers realize with dismay that Matrosova has never been there. "Even if Matrosova had fought her way back to tree line, how could she have traversed this?" Ramos writes. "It took some of the world's best mountaineers two hours to travel a quarter-mile in this terrain. Why would she have abandoned the relatively easy trail to take this on?" Larson, another team member, will say later, "It just didn't feel right to me. She had no business being there."

It has taken the MRS team more than their allotted forty minutes to reach this site, but they clearly felt it was worth their time and effort. Mancini and Holmes have been listening on their radios as the four have made their way down into the drainage, back up the other side, and up the side of Mount Madison. Mancini says, "I was optimistic at the fire department. But while we were standing there, I was not as optimistic. If I'm this cold and uncomfortable and away from my truck for two hours, how is she going to be okay?"

Mancini recalls that conditions were horrendous as the MRS team dropped into the drainage, which further dimmed his own optimism. "It was so thickly wooded, there was snow blowing, you couldn't see well at all, not even the reflections of their headlamps," he recalls. At one point the team is 1,000 yards from the beacon site and taking turns plowing a trough through waist-deep snow. "They made it through a hellacious bushwhack and deep snow. They worked very hard to get there," says Holmes

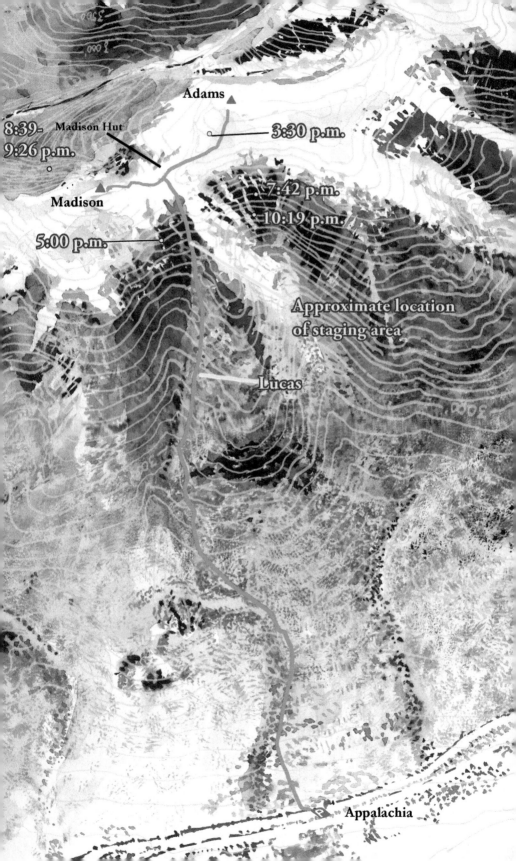

Adams

Madison Hut

8:39–
9:26 p.m.

3:30 p.m.

Madison

7:42 p.m.

10:19 p.m.

5:00 p.m.

Approximate location
of staging area

Lucas

Appalachia

Finding no sign of Matrosova after their difficult trek, Dupuis and his team must make a tough decision. Speaking to Sandy Stott, Dupuis will later outline the problems they are facing and how they choose to respond:

My biggest concern about going any higher was not being able to return to tree line, as the wind would then be in our faces. Also the cold was really sapping our energy at that point. We were in snow at times waist deep and other times fighting through thick scrub which grabbed us at every step. As a team, we had a quick huddle and decided it was time to go down.

Communicating by radio, the six rescuers make a collective decision that Mancini and Holmes can start down while the MRS team begins to backtrack. So, at 12:15 a.m., Mancini and Holmes head down to Appalachia and back to warmth and security. Sitting in his truck, Lucas is following the progress of the attempted rescue. "My optimism dropped when I heard on the radio that the teams were coming down," he says. "If we couldn't go any farther, the chances for [Matrosova] were not good."

At 1:00 a.m., as the first MRS team advises Ober that they have not found Matrosova and are beginning to work their way back, the four members of the second MRS team are stashing the rescue litter on the side of the Valley Way, just above the drainage. They provide Ober with the GPS coordinates of the litter so it can be retrieved the following morning, when the search will be resumed.

By 3:00 a.m., both MRS teams and Mancini and Holmes are all back in the Appalachia parking lot. Ober describes to Stott what he saw as the rescuers emerged from the trailhead: "You could see they were all exhausted. Their neck warmers and faces were crusted with ice. They looked like zombies."

Ober debriefs with each team before they leave for home. Mancini, Holmes, and Lucas are reunited, and because of their exhausting efforts, will not return five hours from now to continue searching. Holmes says in retrospect, "I've been on more miserable rescues, but I've never been on a colder one. You could not sit still. The physical pain of being cold occupied my mind at all times up there."

Mancini recalls the fatigue he felt as he left the parking lot. "I pulled over in Twin Mountain at the State Police barracks to rest my eyes," he recalls. "It was quite a task to drive home. I remember being upset we didn't find her. I really wanted to be there the next morning to participate, but I knew it would have been really risky because I was so tired."

Later, safely home and in the warmth of his own bed, Mancini still has a tough time shaking off the night's ordeal, "I tossed and turned," he says. "I've slept outside in really cold weather—plenty deep in the wilderness with no one close by. You deal with it. But the conditions up there made me question my confidence and ability level. You had to be on your A-game. If you started making bad decisions, taking your gloves off to Jetboil, you had to adjust. I should have never let Matt and Glen get out of my sight. I should have moved slower."

Though by most standards, Mancini has performed competently and admirably, by his own standards, he could have done better—and he realizes there are lessons he can learn from that.

Once everyone has left, Ober is alone in the parking lot, where he has been holding the fort for ten straight hours after a full stint at his day job. At 3:43 a.m., he informs a State Police dispatcher that all units are clear, and rescue efforts will resume at 8:00 a.m.

Ober puts his cruiser in drive and leaves the parking lot. Resisting the urge to go home and sleep, he spends the next few hours driving from trailhead to trailhead. "Maybe she's going to make it out onto Route 16," he hopes. "I'll just go back and forth and see if she pops out of the woods, and I'll pick her up." When it becomes obvious to him that there is no activity anywhere at the trailheads, he returns to the Appalachia command post to prepare for the morning's massive search.

At 6:00 a.m., Ober places a call to AFRCC and receives still more confounding information. Between 2:17 a.m. and 5:27 a.m., the AFRCC received additional beacon hits. But this time, four of them have the same coordinates: those of the very first beacon hit received from Star Lake Trail at around 3:15 p.m. the day before.

Today, maybe this is where they'll find her.

All of the beacon hits Ober had received from AFRCC as of 6:00 a.m., Feb. 16, 2015

2:17-5:27 a.m.

Adams

Madison Hut

Star Lake

3:30 p.m.

8:39-9:26 p.m.

Madison

7:42 p.m.

10:19 p.m.

5:00 p.m.

X
BREACH

"I called to the other men that the sky was clearing, and then a moment later I realized that what I had seen was not a rift in the clouds but the white crest of an enormous wave."

—*Sir Ernest Shackleton, polar explorer*

N.H. Fish and Game Department
Monday, February 16, 2015

PRESS RELEASE
RESCUE UNDERWAY FOR WOMAN ON MOUNT ADAMS AFTER ACTIVATION OF PLB

Search crews from N.H. Fish and Game and Mountain Rescue Service (MRS) searched through the night in fierce winds and frigid temperatures for a hiker who activated her Personal Locator Beacon (PLB) indicating an emergency. The beacon is registered to Kate Matrosova, 32, of New York City. At approximately 3:30 p.m. Fish and Game was made aware of an emergency signal from a personal locator beacon picked up by the Air Force Rescue Center out of Panama City, FL. The beacon signal showed a coordinate between Mount Madison and Mount Adams. Attempts to contact the individual who activated the PLB via her cell and satellite phones were unsuccessful, and a rescue mission was launched with members of the Fish and Game Advanced Rescue team and volunteers from Mountain Rescue Service called into action. The crew hiked over 3 miles to a location north of Mount Madison and searched off trail in deep snow and thick scrub trees in an area identified by the beacon signal as the probable last known location of the distressed hiker. After spending hours searching the area, the crews were unable to locate any sign of the hiker and were forced to suspend the search due to the treacherous conditions. The conditions these rescuers had to contend with were temperatures of -20 degrees F and falling (not factoring windchill), with sustained winds at 60-80 and visibility at 1/16th of a mile. The search will continue in the morning. But wind temperatures will again be challenging factors to the rescuers as they search for the missing hiker.

Mount Washington Observatory
Feb. 16, 2015
5:35 a.m.

Ryan Knapp is looking through a thick glass window at the weather bomb that began the day before and, having detonated, is wreaking havoc on Mount Washington's summit and in the valleys below. A wind gust is clocked at 141 mph. There it is. He and his colleagues haven't seen a gust that big since 2008, when one hit at 145 mph. The temperature on the summit is -20°F with a windchill of -71°F. Winds are from the north and, when not gusting, are sustained at 116 mph. The ground snow is blowing wildly.

They've heard rumors from down below that something is going on. New Hampshire Fish and Game and State Police Dispatch have called a couple of times for weather updates. Has someone not heeded the strong warning Knapp posted almost twenty-four hours before?

Knapp's shift has concluded, but he won't be going to bed anytime soon. Mount Washington always has plenty of interesting weather to watch, and this morning his weather station is setting global records. There'll be time to sleep later.

In about twelve hours, at 5:43 p.m., Knapp's colleague, Mike Dorfman, a weather observer and IT specialist at the Observatory, will capture the full impact and distinction of this weather event in a Twitter posting: "The summit dipped down to 35 degrees below zero last night, tying my personal record for cold temperatures in my time here. As far as I can tell, we were recording the second coldest temperature on Earth for several times last night, second only to the South Pole station in Antarctica. Our windchill, which approached 90 below at its coldest, was the lowest recorded on Earth last night."

N.H. Army National Guard Base
Concord, N.H.
6:50 a.m.

Chief Warrant Officer (CW3) Iain Hamilton walks into the crew briefing room to meet the team he'll fly with this morning. They've gathered after receiving a request for air search support from Sgt. Ober just after 8:00 p.m. the previous night. The crew of four and their ground support team know they're going after a missing hiker near Mount Adams and that the weather is going to pose some serious challenges to that effort. Hamilton, a veteran Blackhawk helicopter pilot who has flown combat missions in Iraq and Afghanistan, has seen difficult conditions before. From his experience on Medivac missions in wartime, he's well versed at flying deep into harm's way and back out again carrying an injured fellow soldier.

Hamilton greets his crewmates, CW2 David Breton (co-pilot), 1st Sgt. Gregory Gerbig (crew chief), and Staff Sgt. Christopher Wareing (flight medic). After receiving an update on the rescue effort from Sgt. Ober, the crew conducts a full mission briefing that includes a review of the extreme weather. This involves a comprehensive discussion between the flight crew and the ground support team about the goal of their mission, the terrain, the weather factors that need to be considered, the amount of fuel they think they will need, and the potential changes that might occur in future weather patterns. The entire briefing could be a lesson in situational awareness, as everyone involved considers all the factors currently in play, what might change along the way, and how all of this might affect their ability to fulfill their goals.

"Air crew coordination pre-, during-, and post-mission focuses on creating an environment where no one is afraid to speak up," says Hamilton. "If someone isn't feeling good about the mission, then somebody else probably isn't either."

Hamilton says that, as the pilot, he commands the mission, but he isn't necessarily the highest-ranking officer on the aircraft. Any member of the crew, of whatever rank, is encouraged to speak up, create a necessary pause, and not feel that he or she must defer to perceived expertise or higher authority. The goal, says Hamilton, is to "create a healthy dialogue among the crew around risk and return." It's an environment unlikely to result in dysfunctional momentum.

At 8:20 a.m., the 16,000-pound Blackhawk helicopter is wheeled out of the hangar and onto the tarmac for its pre-flight check. It is equipped with a high-powered hoist (HPH)—a cable used to lower the medic to the stricken person—and a Forward-Looking Infrared (FLIR) camera designed to detect heat signatures emitting from a human being.

Hays Chart Feb. 15, 2015

This is an image of the chart from the Hays Recorder at the Mount Washington Observatory on Feb. 15, 2015. The red pen lines represent wind speeds measured with a complex system of gauges by a pitot static tube anemometer. When the wind speed increases, the red pen is pushed farther away from the center. If the winds are gusty, the pen responds by recording peaks and valleys. In especially gusty weather, the red line grows thicker over time. The Hays is calibrated to record speeds up to 140 mph. The numbers in the outer rim represent the time of day, the average hourly wind direction, and the hourly average wind speed. You'll note a steady increase in wind speed and gusts during the course of the day. At 1:06 p.m. the Hays graphed a wind gust of 105 mph (signified by the arrow). This occurred nineteen minutes after Kate Matrosova turned around on Mount Adams.

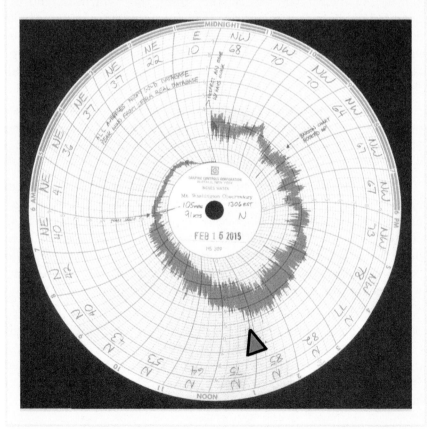

Hays Chart Feb. 16, 2015

This is an image of the chart from the Hays Recorder at the Mount Washington Observatory on Feb. 16, 2015. Note the significant increase in wind speeds and gusts beginning at about 2:00 a.m. At 5:36 a.m., the summit received a wind gust of 141 mph (signified by the arrow). Because of the severity of the readings at the outer rim of the chart, average hourly wind speeds and directions through the morning are displayed in the inner rim. At 1:00 p.m., when rescuers found Matrosova, winds on Mount Washington were averaging 100 mph, with gusts well above that.

Courtesy of the Mount Washington Observatory

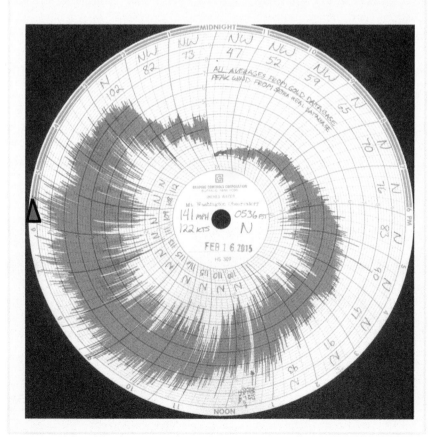

Laconia Municipal Airport
Gilford, N.H.
7:00 a.m.

Col. Bill Moran is shoveling snow. He and his two colleagues are removing a foot and a half of the white stuff that is blocking the front of the air hangar where their Cessna 182 airplane is waiting to depart. Moran and his teammates, Capt. Bruce Determann and Capt. Bruce Neff, are volunteers for New Hampshire Civil Air Patrol (CAP), and they welcome the physical effort because the airstrip is as cold as "a blowing tundra," according to Moran.

Moran received a call at 9:30 the previous night from Fish and Game requesting air search support for the rescue attempt on Mount Adams. Under the memorandum of understanding between New Hampshire Fish and Game and the AFRCC, Civil Air Patrol assets with specialized equipment to track and locate emergency locator beacons can be requested for search and rescue operations. The Cessna currently blocked by deep snowdrifts has onboard directional finder equipment capable of detecting both the 406mhz data burst signal and the low-power 121.5mhz homing signal transmitted by the type of personal locator beacon Matrosova has activated.

At 5:30 a.m., Moran received a follow-up phone call from Lt. Goss at Fish and Game who told him, "I want you to fly now." Goss told him the night before that he'd call between 8:30 and 9:00 a.m. to let him know if CAP would be needed. Obviously Fish and Game isn't wasting any time.

Civil Air Patrol Cessna 182 on the tarmac at Laconia Municipal Airport.

Once a path is cleared to the Cessna, the crew begins its pre-flight check. To ensure that there is no water or ice in the fuel lines, a crew member holds a specially designed glass jar up to the sump located on each wing, where the Cessna's fuel tanks reside. The sump is a small fuel drain that, once depressed, will expel a small amount of fuel into the jar. If there's water present, it will float to the top. Results from one of the two sump tests reveal no water in the fuel. Good. But the second test cannot be immediately completed, because the sump is frozen. The crew will not fly until they're sure there is no water in that line. "We don't need to become part of the search itself," Moran explains.

They try holding a portable quartz heater up to the sump, but that doesn't work. Moran has an idea and calls his wife to ask that she bring her hair dryer to the airport. That handy appliance takes less than five minutes to unfreeze the sump. No water. It's time to fly.

Appalachia Parking Lot
7:00 a.m.

Lt. Wayne Saunders pulls his Fish and Game-issued SUV into the parking lot and up beside the cruiser Sgt. Ober is sitting in. Ober called Saunders, a twenty-year veteran of New Hampshire Fish and Game, at 10:00 p.m. the night before and informed him of the search and rescue mission. Ober told Saunders that while crews were currently on the mountain, Fish and Game was gearing up for the likelihood of resuming the search the next morning.

Saunders approaches his job with some perspective. In 1997, he was shot in the line of duty by a gunman who had just assassinated a district court judge, a newspaper editor, and two New Hampsire state troopers. Saunders was ambushed by the gunman and was shot in his cruiser. Miraculously, the bullet struck his badge, but it still managed to do significant damage as it passed through his biceps and shoulder. The gunman would go on to shoot and injure a U.S. border patrol officer and two more state troopers before he was shot and killed in a deeply wooded area. Saunders would be away from the job he loves, recovering from his wounds, for a year.

Saunders can tell that his sergeant has burned the midnight oil but that, as always, he is completely focused on finishing the mission. Ober brings Saunders up to speed on the events of the previous night, the air and ground assets he has lined up for the day's search, and the updated beacon coordinates.

The winds in the parking lot are strong and frigid. Fish and Game has requested a Mobile Incident Management Vehicle from the New Hampshire Department of Safety's Division of Emergency Services. This vehicle, also known as an Incident Command Post (ICP), is the size of a Greyhound bus and houses technical and other equipment to aid in mission coordination while it keeps those in charge out of the elements. It has a large conference table, a wide-screen video monitor to display maps, a bank of phones and independent lines, and a full dispatch center. Given the extreme conditions, Ober and Saunders decide to move the operation to the Randolph Fire Department parking lot, which is .8 miles away. The new location will allow search and rescue team members to gear up indoors.

New Hampshire Department of Safety Mobile Incident Management Vehicle at Randolph Fire Station on Feb. 16, 2015.

Lt. Goss, a twenty-eight-year veteran of New Hampshire Fish and Game and the agency's search and rescue team leader, arrives at the parking lot almost simultaneously with Saunders and Ober, and the three begin to coordinate the day's mission. Ober has already identified where assets need to be deployed. In a short time, multiple rescue crews will be moving toward them from land and air, and they want to get all that expertise directed to the mountains above them.

If you live in New Hampshire, within an hour or so of the Presidential Range, you are likely awake on this federal holiday as Ober, Saunders, and Goss plan the large-scale search and rescue mission. You aren't sleeping because you've probably been stirred by the extreme winds surging relentlessly against the north side of your house. As you have your coffee, you note that the outside temperature on your thermometer reads -15°F. You are loathing the thought of going into the garage to make sure your generator will start, because you believe there's a 100-percent probability you're going to lose power before this day is over. As you watch the 7:00 a.m. broadcast of WMUR's News 9, you're jarred out of your lingering sleepiness and forced to process the graphic you see on the screen: "MISSING HIKER." When integrated with what you're seeing and hearing outside and the data on your thermometer, you are trying to process this alert, since it's hard to believe anyone would have gone up into the mountains over the past thirty-six hours.

BREAKING NEWS AT 7:00
MISSING HIKER

The newscaster tells you that rescuers are resuming their search for a woman near Mounts Madison and Adams, responding to her activation of an emergency locator beacon that was picked up the afternoon before. Your thoughts go immediately to the missing woman and to the rescuers who are putting themselves into harm's

144

way, for a second day, to find her. The story is hard to understand, you worry for all involved, and you scold yourself for complaining about having to go into the shelter of your garage to test the generator.

Randolph Fire Department
8:00 a.m.

The relationship between New Hampshire Fish and Game and the volunteer search and rescue teams over which the agency has statutory authority is a symbiotic one. Fish and Game cannot possibly manage the hundreds of search and rescue calls it handles each year without the help of these teams, and without Fish and Game, volunteer search and rescue teams and their members wouldn't have the benefits of sponsored training, workers' compensation coverage, and the infrastructure needed to support such missions.

Saunders, Ober, and Goss plan to form four teams, three that they will deploy to the three unsearched areas where a beacon hit has been picked up, and a fourth to serve as a standby crew. Since the second beacon hit at Pine Link was cleared by the Mountain Rescue Service team the previous night, these new teams will need to search Madison Gulf, King Ravine, and Star Lake Trail. Goss gets AFRCC on the phone to "push their buttons," as Saunders puts it. They need a higher degree of probability that one of the beacon hits is the right one.

As rescue personnel arrive, they sign in on Fish and Game's standard Volunteer Search and Rescue Sign-Up Sheet. This document provides Incident Command with the ability to track team members, and also offers validation of participation in the event a rescuer is injured and needs workers' compensation. While members are gearing up, Saunders, Ober, and Goss use the roster to divide the volunteers and Fish and Game SAR personnel into the four teams:

Great Gulf Team

Conservation Officer Jeremy Hawkes (N.H. Fish and Game)

Conservation Officer Delanye Brown (N.H. Fish and Game)

Myles Chouinard (AVSAR)

Hunter Cote (AVSAR)

King Ravine Team

Brian Johnston, Team Leader (Mountain Rescue Service)

Jeff Fongemie (Mountain Rescue Service)

Doug Madara (Mountain Rescue Service)

Eric Siefer (Mountain Rescue Service)

Charlie Townsend (Mountain Rescue Service)

Star Lake Team

Conservation Officer Mark Hensel (N.H. Fish and Game)

Conservation Officer Alex Lopashanski (N.H. Fish and Game)

Mike Pelchat, Team Leader (AVSAR)

Matt Bowman (AVSAR)

Jeremy Broughton (AVSAR)

Anthony Cormier (AVSAR)

Mike Cherim (AVSAR)

Brett Fitzgerald (AVSAR)

Corey Fitzgerald (AVSAR)

Pat Galligan (AVSAR)

Mason Irish (AVSAR)

Erik Thatcher (AVSAR)

Standby Team

Sgt. Brad Morse (N.H. Fish and Game)

Frank Carus, Snow Ranger (U.S. Forest Service)

Paul Cormier (AVSAR)

Diane Holmes (AVSAR)

Matt Schomburg (AVSAR)

Al Sochard (AVSAR)

As the day's rescue effort begins, the Great Gulf Team will deploy to the Madison Gulf Trail, where they will snowshoe in and link up with the Osgood Trail into Madison Gulf and the site of the beacon hits received from there. Conservation Officer Eric Fluette will remain at the trailhead and relay radio transmissions to and from the Incident Command Post and the team.

The King Ravine Team will ascend the Air Line from Appalachia to King Ravine, the site of multiple beacon hits. Because of the highly technical nature of the terrain and the high risk of avalanche, this team of expert alpinists will bring along technical climbing equipment and avalanche safety gear.

The Star Lake Team will ascend the Valley Way from Appalachia to Madison Spring Hut. Once at the hut, they will unlock it and wait inside until the winds calm. Star Lake is the site of the very first beacon hit and several thereafter. All AVSAR members are part of the Winter Above Tree Line Team. Conservation Officers Hensel and Lopashanski will ascend after the AVSAR Team and provide support at Madison Hut.

The Standby Team is a quick-response team that will assist the others if needed or respond to new credible information. Morse and Carus will staff the Incident Command Post to support mission operations until this team is needed out in the field.

Before deployment, all the teams gather for a briefing by the Fish and Game incident commanders. They are shown maps with the different sites of the beacon hits. During the briefing, the commanders strongly encourage them to speak up if at any point they become uncomfortable with the mission and instruct them not to push themselves too hard, given the dangerous conditions. They discuss wind direction and where Matrosova might be bailing off her planned route if she has managed to survive the night.

Chad Miller, the deputy medical examiner for Coos County, and at the time, director of Emergency Medical Services for the Town of Gorham, and his colleague Shawn Costine have brought enough portable radios to outfit nearly every team member. They've also brought extra radio batteries, energy bars, and a large batch of hot soup made earlier that morning by EMT Chris Pyun. Miller will later describe the briefing as "quick and really professional." Rescuers are quiet and focused and make last-minute adjustments to their gear. There's no nonessential chatter. Each person knows what is expected and understands the force of the storm raging above them. Saunders describes the room that morning as "pretty somber, given the circumstances."

During the briefing, AVSAR's Mike Pelchat expresses high confidence that Matrosova is on the Star Lake Trail, the site of the first beacon hit. "I always listen when Mike speaks," says Miller. "I don't know much about his decision process, but he's got so much experience up there, he's usually right. Of all the search and rescue calls I've been involved in with him, I can't remember when he's gotten it wrong."

Later Pelchat will say, "To me, [Star Lake Trail] was the highest probability. She had the wind to her back going up, she turned around, rounded the corner at the col, and got hit by a wall of wind that finished her."

Guides Corey and Brett Fitzgerald, along with guide Erik Thatcher, are on their first AVSAR call. Brett, as yet unfamiliar with the dynamics of search and rescue, recalls getting ready beside his peers. "I was looking around to see what everyone else was bringing," he says. "We were just there to follow instructions. Are people bringing snowshoes? Beacons? Shovels?" His brother also has a vivid memory of the moment. "Even though we were brand new to the team, I knew we belonged there," he says. "Brett and I have a lot of experience in that particular part of the range, so I knew we could contribute to the mission."

At 8:30 a.m., the briefing complete, the teams deploy to their assigned locations, fueled by pent-up energy and anticipation of what the day might hold for them—and for Kate Matrosova.

Army National Guard Base
Concord, N.H.
9:00 a.m.

With Col. Brian Clements providing oversight and Sgt. Diane Cammarata of the Army National Guard offering operational support from the base in Concord, Hamilton and his crew of four lift off from the tarmac and point their Blackhawk helicopter directly north toward the Presidential Range. Just before takeoff, they are joined by Capt. John Wimsatt of New Hampshire Fish and Game, who will accompany them on the flight.

New Hampshire Army National Guard Blackhawk helicopter taking off from base in Concord, N.H.

The craft and crew endure strong headwinds as they make their way northward. Winds are sustained at 80 mph, and the flight is bumpy. As they approach the Sandwich Mountain Range, at 2,000 feet above the ridgeline, the helicopter goes into a sudden, sharp drop. Hamilton's crew chief, Greg Gerbig, is seat-belted in the back and, as the aircraft rapidly loses altitude, he feels his seat drop out from under him. He is rising upward as the aircraft is speeding downward. Gerbig feels his helmet make contact with the ceiling above him. Thankfully, as the aircraft stabilizes and he resumes contact with his seat, he realizes he is uninjured and will emerge with nothing more than a great story to tell.

Hamilton, speaking from the perspective of having flown harrowing missions in combat theaters, will later call the weather that day "the worst conditions I've ever flown in." According to Ryan Knapp, Hamilton and his crew experienced "mountain-induced turbulence." This occurs when strong winds blow perpendicular to—that is, directly at—mountain ranges. As air flows over the top of the mountain and to the leeward side, it produces turbulence that takes the form of updrafts and downdrafts, known as waves. These waves are strongest close to the mountain, which is why the Blackhawk dropped as it neared the ridge.

Under normal conditions, flight time from the base in Concord to the Presidential Range is under thirty minutes. On this day, however, with the 80-mph sustained headwinds, it takes their eight-ton copter fifty minutes to make the trip. The crew arrives in the Madison/Adams area at 9:50 a.m.

Laconia Municipal Airport
Gilford, N.H.
9:00 am

Meanwhile, a second burst of airpower is on its way to the Northern Presidentials. Pilot Moran and his two crewmates take off in their Cessna and point north. The interior of the plane is small, almost claustrophobic. Space is even more limited on this day because of the amount of gear they've brought with them. They have a survival kit on board and extra space blankets if needed. When they check in with Boston Flight Control to report their flight plan, the controller asks if they want the weather conditions for that area. "I think he couldn't believe we were really intending to do that," says co-pilot Bruce Determann, who recalls that they are all wearing "just about everything we own" and the heat is "full on." The crew is wearing long johns, under multiple layers of clothing, and insulated winter boots. The temperature in the cockpit can get up to 80°F, but that day it never gets above 32°F. According to Moran, who has flown bombers and is skilled in flying low-ops missions, the turbulence they are experiencing is happening below 5,000 feet.

Bruce Neff, who will take photographs of the range from the back seat, says, "It was so cold that I packed my down sleeping bag, just in case we went down." Neff will end up taking numerous photos that day. If Matrosova isn't located, the photographs will be shared with CAP volunteers in the hope that such "crowdsourcing" of visual evidence will help locate her.

Determann enters the GPS coordinates to guide them on their 42-mile flight north. Not long into the thirty-minute flight, about twenty miles south of the range, Determann picks up a strong 406mhz signal, a positive sign. "The beacon's antenna must have been pointed straight at us, down the valley, for us to have picked it up that far away," says Determann.

Not long after that, their equipment detects a 121.5mhz homing signal. When he enters the signal frequency into the directional finder, Determann is able to track it to the Mount Madison area. This is another positive development that bodes well for finding Matrosova.

But as the Cessna arrives in the search area, the crew starts to encounter the same severe updrafts and downdrafts that the Blackhawk has experienced. "You could see and feel them," says Moran. The plane loses 1,500 feet of elevation in the downdrafts, and then climbs 3,000 feet with the updrafts.

In response, Moran and his team execute their risk-mitigation plan. "To determine how high we would fly, I added half the elevation of Mount Washington to the elevation of Mount Madison and then added another thousand feet for a risk buffer. The best altitude for a directional finder search is 1,000 feet above the ground. There is no way to fly this at 6,400 feet, with a 6,300-foot mountain to the south and a 5,700-foot mountain directly west. So they decide to remain at the relatively safe altitude of 10,500 feet to conduct their search. When they arrive above the search area, there is so much signal propagation, according to Moran, that they are not able to isolate a valid set of coordinates.

Above Mounts Madison and Adams
9:50 a.m.

As they reach the summits of Madison and Adams, the Blackhawk and Cessna are met with white-out conditions below them. Because of the severe up-and-down drafts and low visibility caused by ground blizzard conditions, the Cessna can't safely drop to the optimal search altitude of 1,000 feet to employ more accurate directional finder or visual search methods. Determann says the strobe of a personal locator beacon "can be seen from a distance of three nautical miles at night. During the day, visibility depends on orientation of the strobe and the amount of contrast with the background." The higher up the Cessna is, the less accurate the reading on the directional finder.

Meanwhile, the Blackhawk is hovering over the summit of Mount Adams. The crew has already searched the north side, but because of the white-out conditions, they are unable to see the ground clearly or make use of the FLIR camera. If they or the ground searchers are even able to locate Matrosova, it will be impossible for the Blackhawk's crew members to lower their medic on the Penetrator cable. If the helicopter is hit by a downdraft in the process, it will slam him into the ground. They search the south side of Adams, and again are unable to see anything.

The Blackhawk has expended a significant amount of fuel during the trip north and the subsequent search. At this point, Hamilton and his crew start a discussion about risk and reward. They consider flying to the Berlin Municipal Airport, located just north of their location in

Aerial photograph of the Northern Presidential Range taken during the search by Civil Air Patrol from an elevation of approximately 10,500 feet. Mount Washington is at the top left, and Mount Madison is the dark shadow near bottom right of photo. Mount Adams is the next peak above it.

Milan, to get more fuel. But then they assess the weather conditions and their inability to provide value to the search effort. As they weigh the risks in full awareness of all the situational factors at play and in the offing, they determine that there is no benefit to continuing with the plan. So at 10:05 a.m., they radio the Incident Command Post that they are returning to their base in Concord. The ride back in the prevailing tailwinds proves to be much faster, and they touch down twenty-five minutes later.

Like the Blackhawk crew, the crew members of the Cessna recognize that they are unable to obtain a consistent set of coordinates, so after an hour and a half of circling the area, they too communicate with the Command Post and turn toward home.

Bruce Determann aptly captures the frustration both crews were feeling as they made the sound but disappointing decisions to abandon their goal: "Unfortunately this search had probably the most extreme conditions, the most complications someone could deal with," he says. Moran echoes Determann's thoughts when he says, "It was very challenging. We've never attempted a homing search in those kinds of conditions. You can't even replicate them for training."

What no one involved in the search and rescue effort could know at the time is that Matrosova put her locator beacon, still flashing, back in her backpack after activating it, which caused the device to give off conflicting signals because it was not optimally positioned. "If the beacon had remained static and properly deployed [facing the sky with antenna extended, as it had been when she fist activated it], that's where we would have found her," says Determann. "Once she folded [the antenna] up and put it in her backpack, all bets were off."

Great Gulf Trailhead
10:00 a.m.

As Conservation Officers Hawkes and Brown and AVSAR team members Chouinard and Cote make their way into Madison Gulf on snowshoes, Conservation Officer Eric Fluette stands by in his cruiser near the Great Glen Ski Trails. Lt. Goss explains that the planning group wants to get a team into the Great Gulf in case Matrosova has made it down over the Star Lake Trail and is coming down the drainage.

Radio coverage in this area is less than ideal, and with multiple searchers heading into the deep wilderness of the Gulf, Incident Command wants a radio relay point between them and those in the woods. Fluette, a five-year veteran of New Hampshire Fish and Game and a member of the SAR team for one year, has his gear with him in case he needs to assist the team he's monitoring. Fluette recalls the morning vividly: "I can remember sitting there and looking up at the summit. There was snow and wind just flying across. I remember thinking about what it must be like above tree line—the gear they'd need and the dangers. It looked like a big wind storm up there."

Incident Command Post
Randolph Fire Department
10:00 a.m.

With the three teams making progress toward their designated search areas, Lt. Wayne Saunders steps away from the Incident Command Post and drives toward Gorham, heading for the Royalty Inn, where Charlie Farhoodi is holding worried vigil. Farhoodi welcomes him inside, and Saunders reviews what has been done up to this point of the search and what is planned for the rest of the day.

He shows Farhoodi a map of all the beacon hits and points out where the various search teams are heading. He explains to Farhoodi that his wife's survivability odds are much greater if she has been able to get below tree line. He also explains that it might be too risky, given the weather conditions, for his teams to venture above tree line that day.

From his spot in Gorham, in the lee of the mountain range, Farhoodi is not aware of how bad the weather is on the exposed areas above tree line in the Presidentials. Saunders explains to him that the clouds they see from their window are actually blowing snow and that the weather is much different—much worse—up there.

Photograph of Mount Madison (left) and Mount Adams (center) taken on the morning of Feb. 16, 2015 by Chad Miller, the deputy medical examiner for Coos County, and at the time, director of Emergency Medical Services for the Town of Gorham. Note the snow blowing off of the summits.

Farhoodi goes over with Saunders what he and his wife were doing as they prepared for the trip, up to the time he dropped her off at the Appalachia trailhead. He shows Saunders photographs of her gearing up for the trip and leaving the Appalachia parking lot to begin her hike. Saunders recalls that, as Farhoodi looked out his hotel window, he seemed very subdued. "I think he knew what was coming," says Saunders. "He was preparing himself and taking in all of the information I was giving him."

Photograph of Kate Matrosova that Charlie Farhoodi provided to Lt. Wayne Saunders, showing clothing similar to what his wife was wearing when she departed Appalachia the day before.

The Valley Way
11:00 a.m.

Over on the Valley Way and Air Line trails, the teams from AVSAR and Mountain Rescue Service are working their way up. The ten-member AVSAR team locates the rescue litter left by MRS2 in the wee hours of the morning. Their ascent has been quiet. "It was so cold, we didn't want to talk on the way up," says Pelchat. The team members are working hard to stay as close together as possible.

Members of Androscoggin Valley Search and Rescue heading up the Valley Way having just retrieved the rescue litter left by MRS2 the night before.

Brett and Corey Fitzgerald are in the midst of their winter "shakedown" hike, except it's happening two weeks early. Brett recalls that conversation was infrequent and informal. "No one really wanted to talk about it," he says. "It was the elephant in the room—if we find her, it's going to be a recovery."

Mike Cherim echoes Fitzgerald's sense of the mood: "We felt we were on a recovery mission and not on a rescue mission. We weren't optimistic. We were somber, but we were doing what we signed up for." For many of them, says Cherim, the mission felt particularly significant, as if all their training and experience had led them to this moment.

As the team gets closer to tree line, Pelchat motions for everyone to stop. Over the next several minutes, the Valley Way will resemble an outdoor equipment store. Team members dig deep in their packs and retrieve insulated shell layers, goggles, mountaineering mittens, food, and liquids. They need to layer, hydrate, and take in as much fuel as they can before entering an environment that will not be conducive to doing any of those things. "When we hit tree line, we were all bundled up—goggles, big jackets," says Matt Bowman. "It wasn't every man for himself, but with all that stuff on, you are in your own world."

Before moving above tree line, recalls Brett Fitzgerald, Pelchat looks at his teammates and says, "We'll test it. If any of you wants to turn around, that's okay." There are no takers.

Pelchat will later explain the process he puts in place at this point to mitigate the risks of taking his team above tree line: "We established a buddy system, where team members would pair up and monitor each other for frostbite and altered mental status. Candor among members is critical. If someone is uncomfortable, cold, or freezing, our plan was to send the affected member back to tree line with a teammate."

It is very clear, as rescue team members recount their thinking on that long day, that whether you're in the cockpit of a Blackhawk or a Cessna, at Incident Command Post, at tree line—or working in a four-story office complex in an urban setting—candor and transparency are critical to managing risk and making good decisions.

With Conservation Officers Hensel and Lopashanski still working up the Valley Way, Pelchat's team is post-holing and breaking trail through 8-to-10 inches of fresh snow above tree line. Those wearing snowshoes move to the front to aid in the process. Brett Fitzgerald and one of his teammates are pulling the litter, when a strong gust of wind picks it up and blows the litter and the two rescuers about 10 feet from the group. They are not injured, however, and the team regroups and continues toward Madison Spring Hut, and shelter from the winds.

Incident Command Post
Randolph Fire Department
Noon

Lt. Jim Goss is making progress in trying to get accurate coordinate information from the AFRCC. But the process hasn't been entirely smooth. "I understand why, but I was getting frustrated with the protocols," he recalls. "You're tired, under stress and pressure, you want answers, and someone's asking you to fill out a form."

But the big stressor for Goss is the safety of the searchers. "It's their decision when they get up there," he says. "I would never tell them, 'You have to go.' They are the first priority. Obviously you want to help the victim, but our guys and the volunteers are number one."

Fatigue is also a factor here. At around 11:00 a.m., Sgt. Ober, who's been on duty for twenty-six straight hours, gets a call from Col. Garabedian. According to Ober, the colonel, who has been receiving regular updates, tells him empathetically, "You need to leave. Go home." Garabedian knows that only a direct order will get Ober to leave the scene. "I wanted to finish it," says Ober. Instead, he collects his things, bids his brethren goodbye and, with heavy eyes, finally drives home to his waiting family.

At last, the AFRCC informs Goss that they're confident the Star Lake coordinates are more probable than any of the other locations. That call sets off a string of rapid adjustments. The Great Gulf Team and Fluette are called back and told to respond to the Appalachia parking lot. The Standby Team is activated and instructed to do the same. Sgt. Brad Morse, who has been at the Incident Command Post, will gear up and meet the incoming teams at Appalachia and start up the Valley Way. The MRS Team heading to King Ravine is in the vicinity of the Star Lake team and is also diverted to the Valley Way. All resources are now being brought to bear on Star Lake.

Madison Spring Hut
Noon

Meanwhile, the AVSAR team is having a bit of a problem. As they huddle together in front of the door of Madison Spring Hut, they are unable to get inside. The locks on all the doors are frozen solid. So they move to the leeward side of the hut to get out of the north wind barreling through Madison Col.

On the summit of Mount Washington, the wind speed is averaging 100 mph and gusting to 125. The temperature is -16°F without the windchill. Pelchat estimates that winds in the col are sustained at 70 mph and gusting to 90.

Although the team is supposed to wait for the winds to ease before moving on, Pelchat senses a window of opportunity in which to move toward the beacon hit. He tells anyone who is too uncomfortable to continue to stay at the hut, but again there are no takers. His plan is to deploy in a line from the hut and sweep across Star Lake Trail to the beacon hit. If they are unable to locate Matrosova, they'll continue a short distance beyond the beacon, regroup, and sweep back toward the hut. "It was really windy and dangerous," says Cherim. "But I didn't feel fear, and I didn't sense that anyone else did either."

Members of Androscoggin Valley Search and Rescue convene on the leeward side of Madison Spring Hut to avoid the winds blasting through the col before deploying to Star Lake Trail in hopes of locating Matrosova.

Pelchat tells the group that there is no way they'll attempt to search higher up on Adams, and that he doesn't want his team to proceed any farther than one-half mile above tree line. He continues to stress the importance of watching out for one another. If the team locates Matrosova alive, they'll cover her with a tent fly and perform life-saving measures until the rescue litter can be retrieved from the hut. If she has not managed to survive, they'll deal with that when they have to.

Members of Androscoggin Valley Search and Rescue making their way on Star Lake Trail toward the site of the first beacon hit. The slope on the right is Mount John Quincy Adams and Mount Adams is in the distance. Note the ground blizzard conditions.

The team leaves the relative shelter of the hut and begins its sweep across Star Lake Trail. As they hike along the Parapet, near Star Lake, they are getting battered. Erik Thatcher is walking along when a strong gust of wind knocks him off his feet, and he finds himself sliding. For the first time in his climbing career, he is called upon to use his ice ax to self-arrest. It's an unusual moment, because he's not on a steep slope; the wind is actually moving him across flat ground. Other team members are forced to kneel between violent gusts of wind.

Later, Cherim will describe the importance of planning for each step: "You'd walk, get blown over, kneel, wait for the wind to ebb, stand up, walk, and get blown over again. It was deliberate movement. You had to think ahead."

At times, team members are reduced to a crawl. Corey Fitzgerald estimates some of the gusts at near 100 mph. Some of the rescuers, including Fitzgerald, are wearing snowshoes. While very helpful in deep snow, in high winds snowshoes can act like sails, and that's exactly what's happening. If a strong gust hits a rescuer in mid-snowshoe step, his legs are whipped around like those of a rag doll.

Pelchat is counting heads as his team passes by Star Lake. Erik Thatcher and Mason Irish approach from behind. As the two carefully descend a rocky slope, each is hit with a massive gust of wind, and they are both shoved violently from the side, as if by an invisible assailant. They are thrown off their feet and narrowly miss falling into large rocks.

Meanwhile, Brett Fitzgerald's neck buff and goggles have frozen. But he won't risk removing his goggles because he is worried his eyes will freeze, so he works to see through the frost. Thatcher, for his part, will cycle through three pairs of goggles.

Androscoggin Valley Search and Rescue Team members on Star Lake Trail. The location of the first beacon hit is ahead and to the left of the first rescuer in the scrub brush. The summit of Mount Adams is barely visible above them.

Unable to read a handheld GPS in the extreme conditions, the team inadvertently passes its destination, the first beacon hit location. A short distance beyond, they find a large rock formation that provides them with some protection from the wind. It's around 12:45 p.m., and they're huddled closely together. A team member checks his GPS and realizes they've gone slightly past the GPS coordinate of the beacon hit. They've been above tree line for an hour, they're extremely cold, and they have endured a total beat-down by Mother Nature with no sign of Matrosova. It's time to work their way back.

This is a series of screen shots from a video taken by Androscoggin Valley Search and Rescue Team member Matt Bowman.

The top image shows three rescuers making their way on Star Lake Trail toward the first beacon hit. Mount Madison is the slope behind them and to the left of the screen. Madison Col is also to the left of the screen. Note the impact the wind is having on the two rescuers making their way down the slope.

The second image shows the impact the winds are having on all three rescuers. Note them leaning into the wind.

The third image shows the two rescuers in the background fighting to maintain their balance.

The final image shows the third rescuer being taken off his feet by the winds. In seconds, the two rescuers in the background will be knocked to the ground. They were uninjured.

XI
RECOVERY

*"Let us squint forward into the storm, knowing there is a
point where the cairns leave off and trails can go no further."*

—*Chip Brown*, Good Morning Midnight

Below Star Lake Trail
12:45 p.m.

One by one, the ten AVSAR rescuers methodically spread out
and down the slope, establishing a line search that will take them back
toward Star Lake and Madison Spring Hut. Slowly, they walk
northward in unison, as an advancing army might do. They are careful
to keep an eye on one another, aware that hypothermia and frostbite
are lurking, and experts are as susceptible as anyone when out in such
conditions. In fact, Mike Cherim and Mike Pelchat are both feeling
the effects of frostbite. Cherim has suffered first-degree frostbite on
his face, and Pelchat has incurred mild frostbite on his fingers from
using his radio. But they keep going.

Unlike his brother Corey, Brett Fitzgerald elects not to wear
snowshoes for the mission. While Corey is battling with the "sail"
effect caused by the winds catching his snowshoes, Brett is in his own
skirmish with Mother Nature. He is post-holing in waist-deep snow
as he moves back toward Star Lake, in much the same terrain as
Matrosova struggled through twenty-three hours earlier.

Thatcher is nearest to Bowman. Like Brett Fitzgerald, he has
forgone snowshoes and also finds himself post-holing through
pockets of scrub trees. Suddenly, Thatcher sees a backpack lying in
the snow about 30 feet ahead of him. There is no one in that vicinity;
the other rescuers are above and behind him. "Is that her pack?" he
yells. Either no one hears him, or the monstrous winds swallow a
reply. As he moves toward the pack, Thatcher scans the area—and
sees her.

Almost simultaneously, Bowman spots the pack from 20 or 30
feet away. "I was totally convinced one of the guys had set his pack
down," says Bowman. He moves closer but doesn't spot Matrosova.
When he approaches the pack, he's confused by what he sees. "I saw
a headlamp on the ground without a strap on it, a little Petzl Tikka,

no strap, just on the ground," he recalls. "A dowel [the selfie stick] was sticking out of the pack. I didn't get it."

Bowman checks underneath the pack to see if Matrosova might be there. "I yanked it up, but there was nothing underneath," he says. "I looked left and right and then I saw her."

Bowman and Thatcher move toward Matrosova. She is lying at an angle on a twenty-five-degree slope, above her backpack. She is pointed in the direction of Star Lake. It is now clear that she was heading back toward Madison and tree line when the end came.

Meanwhile, Mike Cherim is on the high side of the line search. As he works his way back toward Star Lake, he looks downslope and his attention is drawn to someone lying below him. "I thought Brett was down," Cherim recalls. "He was wearing a gray insulated jacket. But when I looked closer, I realized it was Kate." Cherim works his way down the slope toward her, as Thatcher and Bowman arrive at her body. Cherim recalls one of them raising his mountaineering ax to signal the others.

For several members of the team, including Cherim, this is the first time they have seen a dead body, and they feel humbled by the sight. "I had to turn away and catch myself," says Cherim. "I took a deep breath and then got focused on what needed to be done to get her home."

It is 1:00 in the afternoon. Corey Fitzgerald finds a GPS lying on the ground about 15 or 20 feet from Matrosova's body. It is hers, and it lies in a direct line between where she stopped and where her pack is resting. When the incident is reconstructed later, it becomes evident that Matrosova activated her beacon and returned it to the main compartment of her pack. She then left the pack behind and crawled up the slope toward Star Lake. At that point, she left her GPS behind as well, a not uncommon act when one is experiencing the disorienting effects of hypothermia. A short time later, she stopped and would not move again. Death likely followed shortly thereafter.

It is a surreal and solemn moment as the ten battered rescuers stand and kneel before Matrosova's body, amid the storm that ended her remarkable trajectory through life. Bowman turns on his headlamp and illuminates the inside of Matrosova's pack, where he sees her satellite phone and the locator beacon.

When it is fatal, hypothermia offers a glimpse into the victim's final moments. It's an image that is imprinted in the mind of anyone who sees it, an image that will sometimes reappear unannounced, triggered by a similar weather event, a return to the scene, or another rescue. It becomes an unsettling reminder of our own vulnerability.

Matrosova is lying semi-prone on the ground. She is facing upslope toward Star Lake Trail in the shadow of Mount John Quincy Adams, but her upper torso is turned to the left and away from the headwinds. Her right leg is almost fully extended, and her knee is touching the ground. Her left leg is bent and wrapped around a clump of small spruce trees. The area around her is filled with wind-scoured snow. Other than those made by the gathering rescuers, there are no tracks, so it is impossible to discern how she arrived in this awkward, inarticulate, and haunting position.

Her left shell pant leg is unzipped up to her knee, and the strap holding the gaiter to the boot is undone. This is evidence of post-holing. There are small tears on the pants, indicating they may have gotten caught on small spruce trees and rocks. As she was in the "selfies" at Madison Spring Hut, Matrosova is wearing her gray insulated Marmot jacket. The left forearm of the jacket is torn in places, perhaps from scraping against or getting caught on objects in her path. Under this outer jacket is her red-hooded shell jacket. She is wearing every layer of clothing that went with her up the mountain.

Her goggles are on her forehead, and her eyes are open. This is evidence that the lenses of her goggles had frozen over. "Once you start perspiring, your goggles frost up," says Pelchat. "The moisture is really hard to get rid of. The conditions determine whether they're frosted on the inside or outside."

She is wearing a winter hat, her insulated mountaineering gloves with liner gloves underneath, and the neck gaiter that appeared frozen in the selfies. Her right hand is curled up within the glove. It is likely that her insulated gloves were no longer keeping her hands warm enough for the weather conditions. Her left arm is curled and hugging her midsection. Her right arm is curled upward, and its gloved hand is covering her mouth. Her watch is on her right wrist and remains operational. She is in a semi-fetal position, as if trying to retain the last traces of heat in her core. This is consistent with the final stages of hypothermia.

Matrosova's insulated mountaineering mittens remain in the pack, along with her cell and satellite phones, some food, a GoPro camera, maps, itinerary, crampons, a small amount of food, and three 32-ounce Nalgene water bottles, all of which are full and frozen. When he picks it up, Bowman estimates the pack weighs about twenty pounds. The rescuers' packs, by contrast, weigh between fifty and eighty pounds. The mountaineering ax, trekking poles, and tea that Farhoodi told Saunders she took with her are nowhere to be found.

Pelchat radios down to the Incident Command Center to report the recovery. Goss, Saunders, and Miller are in the center. They hear Pelchat's radio call, but the transmission is so scratchy that they are unsure of what he says. They do sense, however, that Pelchat and his team have seen or found something. A couple of anxious minutes pass before Pelchat comes back on the radio and confirms, "We found her."

Pelchat uses an established police radio code to indicate that Matrosova has not survived. Recognizing the team is managing a difficult situation, Saunders waits five minutes before contacting Pelchat again and asking him to confirm Matrosova's passing.

Assistant Deputy Medical Examiner Miller will say later that any lifesaving measures on the part of the rescuers were fruitless at that point. "She was frozen solid," he said. "There was really no question at all that she was dead. The weather was so bad."

Once Pelchat confirms that Matrosova has indeed died, Saunders is ready to notify all those who must have the news, first and foremost, Charlie Farhoodi. Pelchat reports their location, and then advises Incident Command that his team will be working to get themselves and Matrosova out of there as quickly as possible. Photographs of the scene are taken for the accident report, and the team begins its work to bring Matrosova back to Madison Spring Hut.

It is difficult work, physically and emotionally. Team members without snowshoes will post-hole and those wearing them will slide backward on the slope as they break trail through deep snows until they can link back up with the trough they created when they first headed up. "That's when it hit me, when we started bringing Kate back," says Brett Fitzgerald. "The weather was so harsh. You look back, and it's a person there. That's somebody's daughter."

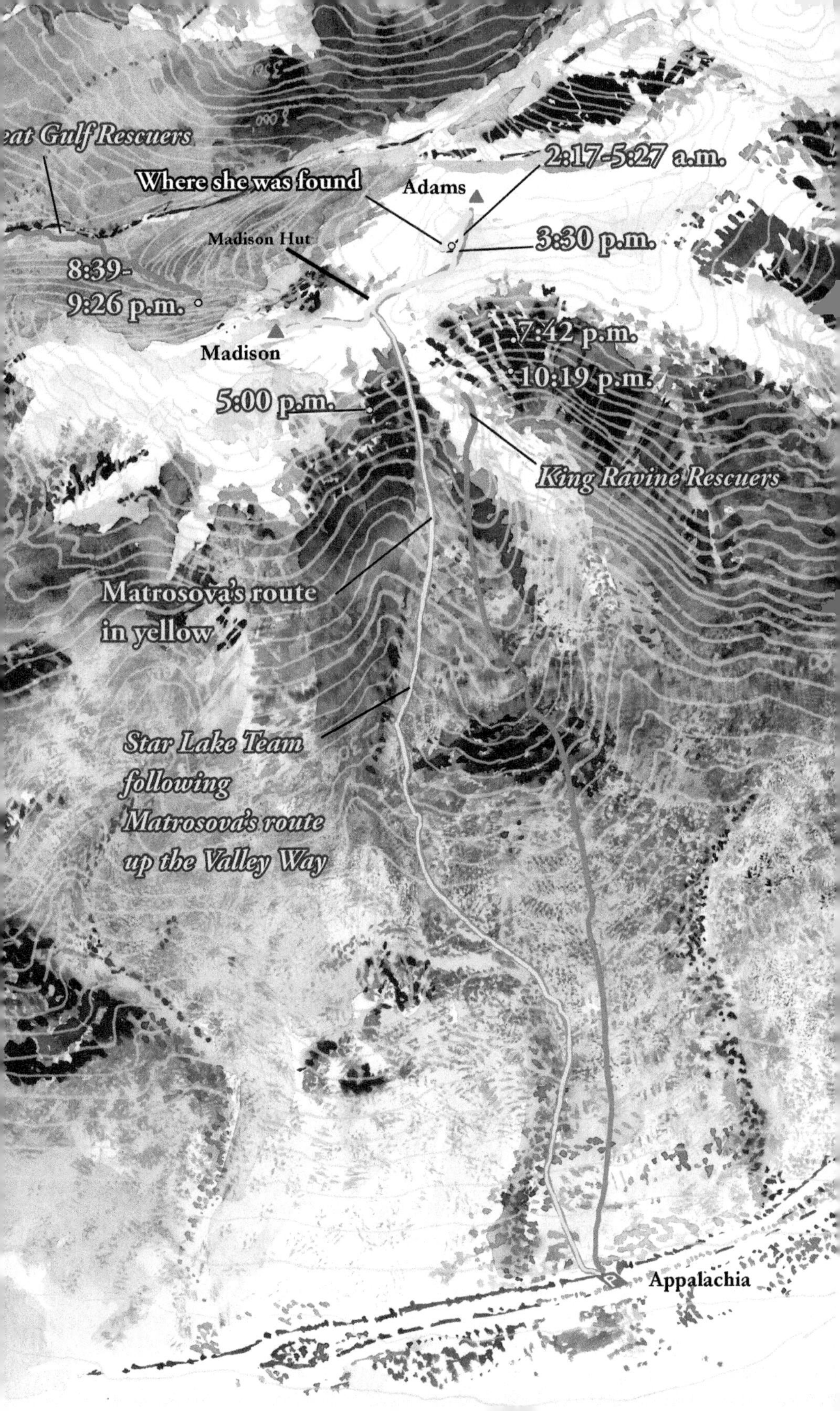

at Gulf Rescuers

Where she was found

Adams

2:17-5:27 a.m.

Madison Hut

3:30 p.m.

8:39-
9:26 p.m.

7:42 p.m.

10:19 p.m.

Madison

5:00 p.m.

King Ravine Rescuers

Matrosova's route
in yellow

Star Lake Team
following
Matrosova's route
up the Valley Way

Appalachia

It takes the team about thirty minutes to return to Madison Spring Hut, where Conservation Officers Mark Hensel and Alex Lopashanski have arrived to assist the freezing and exhausted rescue team. It is very difficult for team members to remove their gloves and expose their bare hands to the extreme cold in order to tie the simple climbing knots that secure Matrosova to the rescue litter in preparation for the walk down. It is a lesson learned, says Pelchat, and something the team will train for going forward.

With Matrosova's body secure, the team of twelve moves out of the leeward side of Madison Hut and into the winds blasting through the col. Lining the front and sides of the rescue litter, they lean forward into the headwinds, and drive themselves down toward tree line. As they approach the trees, where Matrosova first turned on her GPS some twenty-nine hours earlier, they face more than two hours of exhausting work before they will reach her starting point at Appalachia trailhead.

Members of Androscoggin Valley Search and Rescue, Mountain Rescue Service, and New Hampshire Fish and Game on the Valley Way working to bring Kate Matrosova's body back to the Appalachia parking area.

The Mountain Rescue Service team heading to King Ravine, and the Fish and Game/AVSAR team in Madison Gulf are both pulled away from their assignments and, along with the Standby Team, are diverted to assist the team descending with Matrosova. It seems fitting that all the organizations involved in the two-day search—Fish and Game, MRS, and AVSAR—will come together here on this trail to recover a fallen fellow hiker whom they've tried so desperately to save.

Incident Command Vehicle
Randolph Fire Department
Just after 1:00 p.m.

Lt. Wayne Saunders stands inside the Incident Command Post truck and girds himself for what must come next in this process. Lt. Goss is managing the recovery of Matrosova and the descent of the rescue teams from Madison Spring Hut, so Saunders needs to go to Charlie Farhoodi and deliver the crushing news. Chad Miller offers to accompany Saunders to the hotel in Gorham. "I wouldn't send somebody by himself," he says. "I felt like I should go. It can be tough. You never know what to expect; people can react in different ways."

So Miller jumps into Saunders' cruiser, and they make the 6-mile drive to Gorham. It's a sad drive, and there isn't a lot of talk. They've each done this countless times before, but it never gets easier. Upon arriving at the Royalty Inn, they head to Farhoodi's room off a long, dark hallway, and knock. "Can we come in and talk with you Charlie?" Saunders asks when Farhoodi opens the door.

Miller follows Saunders into the room and is shaken by what he sees. On the small desk are roses wrapped in cellophane, chocolates, and a bottle of red wine. "When I saw that, it hit me that it was Valentine's Day weekend," he says. "It threw me off, because I knew I was about to deliver bad, life-altering news."

"Charlie, we found Kate, and she didn't make it," says Saunders gently, after inviting Farhoodi to sit down. Farhoodi sits there in silence. Watching a man's life change in an instant, Miller finds his own eyes welling up with tears. "It was a very somber scene," recalls Miller.

"It's very difficult, but you just have to embrace the silence, and be patient," Miller says. "You feel it's awkwardly quiet, and you want to fill the void, but it's best just to stay quiet." The three sit there as Farhoodi begins to mourn for his wife. Miller senses the news isn't a complete shock to him, that he knew the situation was dire.

"I was concerned for him," says Saunders. "I felt bad about leaving him there alone." But Farhoodi tells them his parents are en route to Gorham and assures them he will be all right and that he will await his parents' arrival. Before leaving, Saunders and Miller again acknowledge Farhoodi's loss, and then return to the Command Post.

Appalachia Parking Lot
4:00 p.m.

Exactly thirty-five hours after she first climbed over the snowbank to begin what would be her last climb, Matrosova approaches the trailhead at Appalachia. Because her body is frozen and set in an awkward position, the rescuers cloak her with a tarp before bringing her out of the wood line and into the parking lot. This area is open and next to a major thoroughfare, and they want to preserve her dignity as best they can.

Again lining all sides of the litter, the rescuers pick it up and walk slowly toward the funeral home's waiting Suburban. The exhausted pallbearers solemnly place Matrosova into the back of the vehicle. Then, having completed their mission, they quietly put away their gear, exchange appreciation and thanks with their fellow teammates, get into their vehicles, and drive back toward their everyday lives of teaching school, operating small businesses, guiding clients, and serving others.

Over the next several days, in addition to his role as director of Emergency Medical Services, Miller will fulfill his other role as assistant deputy medical examiner for Coos County. His examination of Matrosova will reveal no broken bones or fractures or any signs to indicate traumatic injury. His conclusion: "Accidental death due to hypothermia."

Lt. Wayne Saunders types out a press release to inform the public, and to help manage the numerous national and international press inquiries he and Ober will receive over the next several weeks, and beyond.

N.H. Fish and Game Department
February 16, 2015

PRESS RELEASE
MOUNT ADAMS WINTER SEARCH
ENDS IN TRAGEDY

At approximately 2:00 p.m. February 16, 2015, Kate Matrosova, 32, of New York City was located deceased between Mount Madison and Mount Adams in an area near Star Lake. Matrosova activated her PLB (personal locator beacon) at approximately 3:30 p.m. on the previous day. Search and rescue crews were unable to reach her overnight due to extreme wind and subzero temperatures. This morning, the National Guard was able to fly over the area with a helicopter but, due to blowing snow, was not able to see anything. An advance team made of Fish and Game officers, Mountain Rescue Service members, and Androscoggin Valley Search and Rescue members were able to get to the area, braving 108-mile-per-hour winds and subzero temperatures. It appeared that Matrosova had died of exposure to the extreme temperatures.

Epilogue
EMOTION AND REASON

Who is the third who walks always beside you?
When I count, there are only you and I together.
But when I look ahead up the white road
There is always another one walking beside you
Gliding wrapt in a brown mantle, hooded
I do not know whether a man or a woman
But who is that on the other side of you?

—T.S. Eliot, The Waste Land

Summit of Mount Adams
Feb. 8, 2016

I'm not in trouble this time. But I am troubled. I'm on another early February hike above tree line in the White Mountains, but this time it's much different. There's full cloud cover, but visibility is good, unlike it was during my Franconia Ridge hike eight years ago. I can see all the surrounding summits, including those that comprise the Northern Presidential Traverse.

One week from today will mark the first anniversary of Kate Matrosova's death, which occurred not far from where I'm now sitting. I'm on the summit of Mount Adams, perched on a large rock and looking at Star Lake below me. To my right is the imposing summit of Mount Washington. The day's temperature and winds will be markedly different from those Matrosova encountered during her ordeal on this route just under a year ago. I know, because I have been obsessively checking the weather in the days leading up to this hike:

Maximum temp: 21°F

Minimum temp: -1°F

Average temp: 10°F

Average wind speed 29.5 mph

Maximum wind speed: 66 mph

Mounts Lafayette and Adams are my favorite mountains to hike in winter. Their isolation draws me, and I feel a connection to them when I'm up here that I can't explain, even to myself. For the moment,

I'm alone in my thoughts, but I'm not hiking solo today. I'm sitting next to Mike Pelchat, a man I deeply admire and respect. Last year Pelchat, who is manager of Mount Washington State Park, led his Androscoggin Valley Search and Rescue (AVSAR) Team up the Valley Way and across Star Lake Trail to try to rescue Matrosova. He hasn't been up here since that mission. I wonder what he's thinking.

I first learned of Pelchat—and his dedication to helping those who get in trouble in the White Mountains—in the early 1990s when I read an article in *Yankee* magazine by Nicholas Howe called "Fatal Attraction." That led me to Howe's book, *Not Without Peril*, which provides an in-depth analysis of accidents, more than 100 fatal, that have occurred in the Presidential Range and mentions Pelchat as being among the most experienced and knowledgeable of mountain rescuers. To this day, it remains among my favorite books. In fact, when my "Trouble in the Presidentials" presentation concludes, I'm often approached by enthusiastic audience members, asking, "Have you read *Not Without Peril?*"

For more than two decades, whenever an accident happens in the White Mountains and finds its way into news accounts, I've seen Mike Pelchat's name, along with that of Rick Wilcox, co-owner of International Mountain Equipment, another accomplished climber and first-responder I deeply respect. When a mountain accident is reported, Pelchat and Wilcox are either among the rescuers or called upon to provide expert analysis of the incident. I reached out to Pelchat less than a year ago while doing research for my presentation, and he offered to accompany me on a winter hike that would retrace Matrosova's route to Adams.

So, at 8:30 a.m. this morning we plan to meet at the Appalachia parking lot. I'm pretty anxious on the one-hour drive to meet him. But I am also in a lot better shape than I was eight years ago on the Franconia Ridge, which is essential because Pelchat has a legendary reputation for moving through the mountains the way Pelé used to glide over a soccer pitch.

In my anticipation, I arrive at Appalachia early. As I sit in my car, I can't help but imagine Kate Matrosova and Charlie Farhoodi saying their goodbyes. She, happy and excited at what lies ahead, and her husband feeling a tinge of anxiety as he watches her climb up and over the high snowbank. Farhoodi told journalist Chip Brown that his wife considered her Northern Traverse to be a kind of early celebration for the receipt of her American citizenship, another one of her cherished goals. In fact, she received notice after her death that her citizenship exam had been scheduled for April.

I can also picture Mark Ober sitting in his idling cruiser later that night, illuminated only by the headlights of his truck and the dome light inside the cab. I marvel at the resources he was able to marshal and the decisions he needed to make. He was calm and professional. While he certainly felt a deep sense of urgency, he didn't make Matrosova's emergency his emergency. To do so would have infused a shot of emotion into the moment and, perhaps, impaired his judgment. He knew his only chance to help was to stay rational. Finally, I imagine the rescuers, taking their cue from Ober and heading up into the darkness, and the storm it cloaked.

Pelchat arrives, and breaks my train of thought. Time to go. As we make last-minute gear checks, he briefs me on our plan. We'll ascend the Valley Way and attempt to summit Mount Adams. Along the way, we'll test portable radios that we hope to acquire for the AVSAR team through funding from Coos County. We'll also be retracing a large portion of Matrosova's route.

I've been spending a lot of time talking with people about Matrosova's route in my presentations. People find her story powerful and compelling, and they ask many questions of me in hopes of finding some definitive answers about what led to this unsettling tragedy. As I crafted the presentation and its purpose, Charlie Farhoodi was generous with his time and forthcoming about the way that devastating weekend unfolded for him. His courage during our lengthy conversation inspired me, and his warm and steady manner served to ease the anxiety I carried into our conversation. I have felt a deep responsibility to my audiences, and especially to Kate and Charlie, to get this right, to do this well. The more I stood in front of audiences and recounted Matrosova's final steps, the more I'd begun to feel the need to take those steps myself.

Pelchat hasn't seen the path Matrosova took, so the route that led her to where he and his team found her is still a mystery to him. I have loaded her GPS track into my own GPS so that Pelchat and I can get a better sense of where she went that day.

Pelchat identifies our bailout points in the event we encounter white-out conditions above tree line. Given the weather warnings emitting from our portable radios, this is entirely possible, but I trust Pelchat's ability to navigate the area, regardless of visibility. He explains that our primary bailout is Gray Knob Cabin, the first of Matrosova's six planned options which, in her case, turned out to be unreachable.

As we approach the trailhead, it is broad daylight. No need for a headlamp. There is no six-foot snowbank to hurdle, since this winter is much milder than the last. We'll contend with a lot of ice on the trail and on the rocks above tree line, so spikes are in order, but the start of the Valley Way is pretty flat and enjoyable.

Before long, the yellow ATTENTION sign welcomes us into the wood line beyond the Presidential Rail Trail. The trip up is straightforward, and we quickly establish a flow. Depending on our level of exertion, we talk here and there. The Pelchat legend is proving to be true: he moves over the terrain with complete mastery, lightly and smoothly, as if he were born to these hills.

My pack is fully loaded for just about every contingency. I can shelter and stay out overnight if need be. Although we're not planning to hike through avalanche terrain, I've got a beacon, a probe, and a shovel on board. The weight proves challenging, but I realize before long that I'm experiencing an eerie sensation that is becoming even more challenging. I'm not one for superstition; I consider myself to be a rational person. But I feel a presence with us. All the research I've done, the people I've talked with, and the details I've learned about Matrosova and her ordeal are converging to create the feeling that Pelchat and I are not alone today.

As we move along, Pelchat points out more touchstones in the Matrosova story. He shows me the spot Bob Mancini and Matt Holmes staged to await the first MRS team, both trying desperately to stay warm and keep hypothermia at bay. We look over at Pine Link, where the second beacon hit was detected, then across the valley and down into the drainage where Steve Dupuis and his teammates dropped into the deep, black abyss. At this point in my research, I don't have a full grasp of what the rescuers were going through. I'm also unaware of the personal battle Glen Lucas was waging, as he lay in his bivy-bag, curled up against one of the trees we are walking by.

Soon we break tree line and pass the second yellow warning sign. This is where Matrosova first turns on her GPS, and I can now see her track on my small screen. Arriving at Madison Spring Hut, we rummage in our packs for something to eat and drink and for a few extra layers of clothing to repel the approaching cold. It's really icy, and as I collect the gear I've scattered while unloading supplies from my pack, I find myself sliding around awkwardly.

Another weather alert comes over the radio: a snowstorm is possible for the higher summits. It's still overcast, but we can see the tops of all the surrounding peaks. As we prepare to head over to Adams, Pelchat and I are standing at the same intersection Matrosova reached a year ago. Unlike her, we are not going to summit Mount Madison today. Unlike her, we can see the summit of Adams a mile away. Unlike her, we're not being pushed and shoved by winds entering and exiting the narrow Madison Col. And unlike her, we are a number greater than one.

Pelchat and I turn left and walk onto the Star Lake Trail. This will be my first time approaching Adams from this side of the mountain. I find Star Lake to be much smaller than I imagined. It is frozen solid and, as Matrosova did, we walk around it and reach the area where she took her eight-minute pause. While it does seem like a natural place to stop and get some relief from the wind, it just adds to her mystery. I'm wondering what she was doing there.

As we ascend the steeper slopes of Adams, Pelchat has some serious momentum going. Moving briskly up the rocky, ice-glazed trail, he's found a "zone." At the same time, I'm realizing that my situational awareness is a bit impaired. I'm slowing down at the point where Matrosova veered to the right and took a steeper, more direct line toward the summit. As my eyes move intermittently from the GPS to the slope she ascended, I feel a strange sense of dread. What I see on that slope is a desolate place. There is not a lot of snow there today but, rock-strewn and gray, it resembles the surface of the moon. It feels completely removed from the surer environment of the established trail she left behind. I imagine her there, and it's so unsettling that I don't linger long.

Pelchat's fluid climbing and my daydreaming have put some distance between us. He waits as I catch up and show him Matrosova's track, which is now different from our own. Higher up near the summit, we climb up a short, steep slope rising out of a gully. As I climb, I'm blasted from below by a sudden, strong gust of wind, and I realize I'm in a natural wind tunnel. It feels random and takes me by surprise, because it has not been a windy day. It's loud and exciting and carries me up out of the gully—a pretty awesome, if eerie, experience.

Big surprise: Pelchat is waiting for me on the summit. This place is like home for him. He has spent most of his life on this range. We sit for a while, and as he points out various landmarks—speaking of them as if they are friends—we talk about work and family and the mountains. We do not bring up Matrosova's story.

We start our descent of the Star Lake Trail, and I'm finding it a challenge. The ice-covered rocks make for a difficult walk down. At one point, I tilt way beyond my center of gravity and stare down at a pile of boulders waiting for me to pay an unplanned and uncomfortable visit. Somehow, I manage to regain my equilibrium and avert what surely would have been a troublesome fall.

As Pelchat approaches the spot where Matrosova chose a trail less traveled, he seems a bit startled and tells me he thinks he has seen someone standing at the periphery of his vision. He tells me this happens to him in the Whites from time to time, especially on the summit of Mount Washington, where he works. I believe him. And it's something of a relief for me to hear him echo a bit of what I've been thinking and feeling.

We walk on and reach the point where Matrosova took her fateful right-hand turn down into the terrain trap. Even with much less snow, a trap is exactly what it looks like. We don't even try to drop down to follow it because of the ice and the thick patches of small spruce trees that stand ready to hook our jackets and open up new air holes in them. I can't imagine how difficult it must have been to navigate once Matrosova found herself down in it.

Finally, we stop above the slope where Pelchat and his team found Matrosova. He points to the spot. We don't say anything. I pay my respects, and I can only imagine what Mike is feeling.

We continue walking back toward Star Lake and Madison Col. At Madison Spring Hut, we stop briefly to remove a couple of layers, and then head down to tree line. As we dip below the lunar expanse, I can still see the tops of the trees lining the ridge above me. It feels strange to go—as if we are leaving something behind.

The winds are ramping up. From above, I hear a sound—a long, low, loon-like cry that starts softly, strengthens, and then fades away. I slow my descent and look back toward the col. It happens again, sounding closer this time. Sadness takes over, making me feel that we're leaving something behind that doesn't want to be left. I realize I'm standing at my own intersection of emotion and reason. My rational side tells me I'm just hearing the increasing winds as they move through the trees and across the terrain. My emotional side...? Well, I just let the feelings in without trying to find words to explain them. As I turn my back to the col and make my way down, I say my goodbyes to Kate.

Afterword
RESCUERS REFLECT

"I know she was very capable, confident, and an extraordinary human being, but those conditions would make even the most capable person inadequate, even the best mountaineers."
—Bob Mancini (N.H. Fish and Game)

"With all this technology today, the same thing that was killing people in the mountains a hundred fifty years ago, is still killing them today. You can't take the human factor out of it. I felt for Charlie, Kate's husband. I understood he was one of the true victims here, and what he had to go through. I feel for the ones left behind, who day to day, hour to hour, have to live with the ramifications of the decision their loved one or friend made."

—Matt Holmes (N.H. Fish and Game)

"It was really interesting to me to read about her afterward. To have seen my side of things and to learn more about her as a person, the adventurer, coming to America, all the adversity she had to overcome. For Charlie there's a void. She filled the room, and now the room is empty."

—Chad Miller (Director of EMS/Asst. Deputy Medical Examiner)

"When someone dies in an incident like this, it is all too easy for assumptions we make to be ones that explain her death, and why the one passing judgment would not have died in a similar situation. It's part of our human complex that makes us feel invincible, and we fill in the gaps of the story in such a way that explains to ourselves why this wouldn't happen to us."

—Erik Thatcher (AVSAR)

"It's so easy to Monday-morning quarterback, so judgmental. It could happen to any of us. If you get into trouble in the Presi's, you're immobilized. I'm very empathetic."

—Corey Fitzgerald (AVSAR)

"If you take the judgmental approach, you're not reflecting on your own decisions. If you're not willing to do that, you just say she made bad decisions, she died, no empathy. It's easy and lazy to do that. It could happen to any of us. I feel bad for her, for Charlie, and her family."

—Brett Fitzgerald (AVSAR)

"We never knew her, but she's our sister and it's the family that we're concerned about. We said we're taking her down, bringing her home."

—Mike Pelchat (AVSAR) to *Union Leader's* John Koziol

Acknowledgments

While the writing process was a solitary one for me, everything that led up to and followed my putting words to paper was done with the immense support of others, and for that I am grateful to so many people and institutions.

Kate and Charlie: Your story is about so much more than the singular event that resulted in a remarkable life cut short. Thank you, Charlie, for our conversation and for allowing me to use the photos of Kate. I hope you will find some solace in the fact that thousands of people have heard and read about it, and that she is having a positive impact on many.

The Law Enforcement Division of the New Hampshire Fish and Game Department: Col. Kevin Jordan; Col. Martin Garabedian (Retired); Lt. Wayne Saunders; Lt. Jim Kneeland; Lt. Jim Goss (Retired); Sgt. Mark Ober; Sgt. Brad Morse; and Conservation Officers Matt Holmes, Bob Mancini, Glen Lucas, and Eric Fluette.

The Androscoggin Valley Search and Rescue Team and Board of Directors: Special thanks to team members Matt Bowman, Erik Thatcher, Mike Cherim, Corey Fitzgerald, and Brett Fitzgerald. Heartfelt gratitude to Mike Pelchat for your support, wisdom, and willingness to retrace Kate's route.

Mountain Rescue Service: Steve Dupuis and Rick Wilcox.

The New Hampshire Civil Air Patrol: Col. Bill Moran, Capt. Bruce Determann, Capt. Bruce Neff, and Maj. Penny Hardy.

The New Hampshire Army National Guard: Chief Warrant Officer (CW3) Iain Hamilton and Lt. Col. Gregory Heilshorn.

United States Air Force, Book Support Division: Tim Jenkins.

The New Hampshire State Police, Troop F–Twin Mountain, and

Lt. Gary Prince for facilitating contact with Dispatcher Garrett Stevens.

The Mount Washington Observatory staff, especially Senior Meteorologist/Weather Observer Ryan Knapp, who helped me interpret and articulate the treasure trove of weather data that helped me paint the picture of the weather conditions in this story. Thanks also to Director of Marketing and Events, Krissy Fraser, for handling interview logistics, and Sharon Schilling, Obervatory president, for her generosity.

The New Hampshire Public Risk Management Exchange (Primex) Board of Trustees and staff: Thank you for your support, and for your commitment to service and excellence.

Conrad Klefos and Cathy Lunn at the Royalty Inn in Gorham, N.H., for providing background.

For your valuable help along the way: Pam Bales, Michelle Barton, John Boyle, Chip Brown, Alan Clark, Brittni Gorman, Dr. Murray Hamlet, Todd Johnstone-Wright, Sam Kilburn, Kenneth Krause, Chad Miller, Geoff Smith, Sandy Stott, Chris Thayer, and Bill Yeo.

Ron Reynolds, my former industrial arts teacher and good friend, who introduced me to climbing. I'm grateful for the life lessons you provided in the classroom, on frozen waterfalls, and on frigid alpine routes. You taught me much about self-confidence, creativity, and life outside my comfort zone and helped me understand that sometimes the right call is to bail out.

Lucille Stott: I am forever grateful for your support and your patience, and for creating an environment of learning and reflection. You are exceptional at what you do, and I am so glad Sandy told me about this "really good editor" he knew. He was absolutely right. Thank you for your guidance and friendship.

Ted Walsh at TMC Books: Your creativity and vision provided

my initial presentation with a stronger connection to the story, and I'm glad our work could continue on this project.

Caroline Alexander for encouraging me, many years ago, to continue my writing. It took some time to do so, and I'm so honored to have your name and prose as a part of this book. Thank you for your friendship.

My family: Your love, patience, and support over my lifetime have been essential and grounding for me. You watched me dive headfirst into this project and, thankfully, you reminded me that coming up for air every once in a while was essential. For my dear wife, who after reading the manuscript, felt the book should be dedicated to Kate and Charlie, and the rescuers.

I assume full responsibility for any errors. I put forth my very best effort to tell this story in the manner it so rightfully deserves. I talked to many experts, some who were directly involved and others who were not. As I wrote, I drifted into their lane in an attempt to strengthen the story. If I got any of the technical details wrong, I humbly apologize. If I fell short in any aspect of my attempt here, I am a glaring example of the fallibility and vulnerability that exists in each of us.

Selected Bibliography and Further Reading

Adams, Laura. "Avalanche Judgment and Decision Making, Part I." *The Avalanche Review* 24, no. 2 (2005): 9–11.

—"Avalanche Judgment and Decision Making, Part II: The Influence of Human Factors." *The Avalanche Review* 24, no. 3 (2006): 5–9.

—"Avalanche Judgment and Decision Making, Part III: Developing Expertise." *The Avalanche Review* 25, no. 1 (2006): 16–18.

American Alpine Club (various editors): Since 1948, the American Alpine Club has published an annual review entitled *Accidents in North American Mountaineering.* Current and past postings are available online at http://publications.americanalpineclub.org.

Baranoff, Etti, et al. *Risk Assessment* 1st Edition. American Institute of Property Casualty Underwriters, 2005.

Barton, Michelle A., and Katharine M. Sutcliffe. "Learning When to Stop Momentum." *MIT Sloan Management Review,* Spring (2010)

Brown, Chip. "The Trader in the Wild." *Bloomberg BusinessWeek*, May 2015.

Cowan, Neil. *Risk Analysis and Evaluation.* Global Professional Publishing, 2005.

Crickette, Grace, et al. "Exploring Risk Appetite and Risk Tolerance." Risk and Insurance Management Society (RIMS), Executive Report (2012).

Endsley, Mica R., and Daniel J. Garland. *Situation Awareness Analysis and Measurement.* Mahwah, NJ: Lawrence Erlbaum Associates, 2000.

Endsley, Mica R. "Toward a Theory of Situation Awareness in Dynamic Systems." *Human Factors: The Journal of the Human Factors and Ergonomics Society*, 37 (March 1995): 32–64.

Gawande, Atul. "Failure and Rescue," *The New Yorker.* June 2, 2012.

Gonzales, Laurence. *Deep Survival: Who Lives, Who Dies, and Why.* New York: W.W. Norton & Company, 2017.

Howe, Nicholas. *Not Without Peril: 150 Years of Misadventure on the Presidential Range of New Hampshire.* Boston: Appalachian Mountain Club Books, 2010.

Hubbell, D.O., Franklin R. *Wildcare: Working in Less Than Desirable Conditions And Remote Environments.* Conway, NH: TMC Books LLC/Stonehearth Open Learning Opportunities, 2014.

Kahneman, Daniel. *Thinking, Fast and Slow.* New York: Farrar, Straus and Giroux, 2015.

Kamler, M.D., Kenneth. *Surviving the Extremes: A Doctor's Journey to the Limits of Human Endurance.* New York: St. Martin's Press, 2004.

Kick, Peter. *Desperate Steps: Life, Death, and Choices Made in the Mountains of the Northeast.* Boston: Appalachian Mountain Club Books, 2015.

Klein, Gary, and David Klinger. "Naturalistic Decision Making," *Human Systems IAC Gateway.* Winter 1991: 16–19.

Krakauer, Jon. *Into Thin Air: A Personal Account of the Mt. Everest Disaster.* Toronto: Villard Books (Random House), 1997.

Lewis, Michael. *The Undoing Project: A Friendship That Changed Our Minds.* New York: W.W. Norton & Company, 2017.

Perrow, Charles. *Normal Accidents: Living With High-Risk Technologies.* Princeton, NJ: Princeton University Press, 1999.

Roberto, Michael. "Lessons from Everest: The Interaction of Cognitive Bias, Psychological Safety, and System Complexity," *California Management Review.* Fall 2002: 136–158.

Shultz, Kathryn. "Into Thin Error: Mountaineer Ed Viesturs on Making Mistakes," *Slate.* June 14, 2010.

Stott, Sandy. "Too Cold," *Appalachia*, Winter/Spring, 2015: 11–22.

—Stott, Sandy. "Looking for Kate," *Appalachia*, Summer/ Fall, 2016: 64–79.

Taylor, Kelsey. "Keeping Warm: A Discussion with Dr. Murray Hamlet on Cold Weather Physiology." Harvard University Graduate School of Arts and Sciences Blog. March 1, 2013.

Photo and Illustration Credits

A special thank you to those who provided me with images for the book. Their contributions have added greater depth and perspective to the story.

Charlie Farhoodi, husband of Kate Matrosova
- Pg. 1
- Pg. 51
- Pg. 52

Ryan Knapp, Senior Weather Observer/Meteorologist/Photo Administrator at the Mount Washington Observatory
- Madison/Adams photo opposite Contents page
- Pg. 7
- Pg. 21
- Pg. 85
- Pg. 111

N.H. Fish and Game Department: Law Enforcement Division
- Pg. 9
- Pg. 155 (original source: Charlie Farhoodi)

Erik Thatcher, Androscoggin Valley Search and Rescue Team, Mooney Mountain Guides
- Pg. 18
- Pg. 83

Brittni Gorman, Northeast Mountaineering
- Pg. 19

Corey Fitzgerald, Androscoggin Valley Search and Rescue Team, Northeast Mountaineering
- Pg. 92

Glen Lucas, Conservation Officer, N.H. Fish and Game
- Pg. 126

Matt Holmes, Conservation Officer, N.H. Fish and Game
- Pg. 127

Civil Air Patrol, New Hampshire Wing, and especially Bruce Neff
- Pg. 140
- Pg. 151

Lt. Wayne Saunders, N.H. Fish and Game
- Pg. 142

New Hampshire Army National Guard
- Pg. 148

Chad Miller, Gorham, N.H., EMS Director
- Pg. 154

Mike Cherim, Androscoggin Valley Search and Rescue Team
- Pg. 156
- Pg. 159
- Pg. 170

Matt Bowman, Androscoggin Valley Search and Rescue Team
- Pg. 160
- Pg. 161
- Pg. 162

Dreamstime stock photo image by Kmsmith8
- Pg. ix

All illustrations originally created by T.B.R. Walsh for Primex[3] for use in the presentation "Trouble in the Presidentials: What a mountaineering accident can teach us about decision making and managing risk." Used in this publication with the permission of Primex[3].

T.B.R. Walsh and TMC Books LLC created the maps on pages 28, 110, 130, 133, and 169 specifically for use in this book.

Ty Gagne is chief executive officer of New Hampshire Public Risk Management Exchange (Primex[3]), a public entity risk pool serving local governments in New Hampshire. He is a Certified Wilderness First Responder, and serves on the Androscoggin Valley Search and Rescue Team and Board of Directors. He lives in New Hampshire with his wife.

Caroline Alexander is a renowned author of many books, including *The Endurance: Shackleton's Legendary Antarctic Expedition*, and *The Bounty: The True Story of Mutiny on the Bounty*.